El Charro Café
COOKBOOK

THE FLORES FAMILY'S

El Charro Café
COOKBOOK

JANE & MICHAEL STERN
With Recipes by Carlotta Flores

RUTLEDGE HILL PRESS™
Nashville, Tennessee

A DIVISION OF THOMAS NELSON, INC.
www.ThomasNelson.com

To Ron and Marcia Spark

Recipes and foreword copyright © 2002 by Carlotta Flores

Copyright © 2002 by Jane and Michael Stern

Photos courtesy of Ray Flores on pages iii, xiv, xv, 3, 33, 49, 65, 104, 105, 111, 112, and 124
and in the color insert unless otherwise noted.

Photos by Lois Ellen Frank on pages 86, 192, and 193.

Published by Rutledge Hill Press, a Division of Thomas Nelson Inc.,
P.O. Box 141000, Nashville, Tennessee 37214.

Library of Congress Cataloging-in-Publication Data Available

1-55853-992-1

Printed in the United States of America

02 03 04 05 06 — 5 4 3 2 1

CONTENTS

Foreword (*Prólogo*)   vii

Acknowledgments (*Asentimiento*)   viii

Introduction (*Introducción*)   ix

BREAKFAST (*Desayuno*)   5

APPETIZERS (*Aperitivos*)   11

BREAD (*Pan*), **TORTILLAS & TAMALES**   19

SOUPS (*Sopas*)   37

RICE, PASTA, BEANS & VEGETABLES
(*Arroz, Fideos, Frijoles y Verduras*)   53

SAUCES & SPICES (*Salsas y Especias*)   75

SALADS (*Ensaladas*)   99

FISH, CHICKEN & BEEF
(*Pescado, Pollo y Carnes*)   117

DESSERTS (*Postres*)   153

DRINKS (*Bebidas*)   175

ALCOHOLIC BEVERAGES
(*Bebidas Alcohólicas*)   183

Glossary (*Glosario*)   201

Index (*Indice*)   205

FOREWORD

THREE GENERATIONS of the Flores family have steered El Charro through 80 years of good times and hard times. We often think that El Charro runs our lives more than we run it. With corporations gulping down small, family-owned businesses every day, we find this notion both comforting and challenging.

Each generation has created some part of El Charro—from the décor to the menu; from the catering business to adding businesses; from online product sales to the most recent addition, a coffee bar. Now, with a fourth generation coming into the leadership of El Charro, I expect even more exciting changes to this venerable old icon of Tucson.

While working with Jane and Michael on this cookbook, we created several new recipes to celebrate our 80th anniversary. While retelling the stories of El Charro, it brought back great memories of the imagination, the passion, and the wonderful food made by my great-aunt Monica. It also reminded us of the place that El Charro holds in Tucson history—only 2 or 3 businesses remain from the year 1922 when my aunt first opened her doors and sold an entire meal for 15 cents.

Managing El Charro would not be possible without the help of my children; Raymon, Marques, and Candace. My mother, sisters and brother-in-law, Amanda, my nieces, and my husband, Ray, nurture and love El Charro as much as I do. Without them, it would not have the distinctive tastes, traditions, and originality that leads people to our door year after year.

Thank you Jane and Michael for recognizing this grand old restaurant and sharing your love of El Charro with the rest of America.

—Carinosamente Carlotta Dunn Flores and family

(P.S. Thank you Charlotte!)

ACKNOWLEDGMENTS

JANE AND MICHAEL STERN thank all the Flores family for maintaining a great culinary legacy and making El Charro Café such a joyful place. In particular, we are grateful to them for generously sharing their time and knowledge to help fill this book with the color, talent, creativity, and tradition that define their extraordinary restaurant.

We never hit the road without our virtual companions at *www.roadfood.com* — Steve Rushmore Sr. and Stephen Rushmore, Cindy Keuchle, and Marc Bruno — who constantly fan the flames of appetite and discovery along America's highways and byways.

Rutledge Hill Press has proven to be a wonderful literary home for us and for this series of cookbooks from our very favorite restaurants. Larry Stone, Geoff Stone, Bryan Curtis, and Roger Waynick are like great dinner companions, always thought-provoking and encouraging.

And it is a pleasure for us to thank agent Doc Coover for her tireless work on our behalf, as well as Jean Wagner, Mary Ann Rudolph and Ned Schankman for making it possible for us to travel in confidence that all's well at home.

INTRODUCTION

AT EL CHARRO CAFÉ, you eat Mexican. Tucson-Mexican to be exact, which is not Tex-Mex, not New-Mex, and certainly not fast-food-franchise-Mex. Your meal explodes with flavor in a place as colorful as an Aztec kaleidoscope. Mariachi music pulses through dining rooms where the walls are festooned with broad caballero hats and bullwhips, holy images of the virgin saint, and hyper-romantic calendar art on which Aztec gods and gorgeous mortals fight, swoon, and sacrifice. The smells of hot flour tortillas and spiced beef swirl through the air and mingle with the perfume of icy Margaritas from the adjoining Bar *¡Toma!*

This magical experience was set in motion eighty years ago when young widow Monica Flin opened a one-room neighborhood eatery named El Charro Café. Daughter of a stonemason who had come from France to carve a church portal in the mid-nineteenth century, Monica reigned at El Charro into the 1970s, and through the decades she made her café as symbolic of Tucson as the saguaro cactus. El Charro opened only ten years after Arizona became a state, and while the city has grown and Mexican-style fare is now popular throughout the nation, El Charro remains unique. Located in the old home that Monica's father built of black volcanic rock, El Charro defines the Mexican restaurant of the American Southwest. To eat here is to savor not only flour tortillas and towering *topopo* salads (named for the Mexican volcano that inspired them), but also the culture of a town with a vibrant personality, and the heritage of a family who has done so much to define that town.

Older than Los Angeles, Tucson always considered itself Mexican; long before Arizona became America's forty-eighth state, it had established its own Mexican cuisine influenced by French and Spanish cooks who had come north, Pima Indians who had occupied the Sonoran Desert for centuries, and a handful of Anglos venturing to the frontier.

While it is sometimes said that Tucson's culinary ways reflect the traditions of the state of Sonora in northwestern Mexico, many of the town's food-savvy citizens see it the other way around. A century ago, even two centuries ago, Tucson was a cultural center where Sonoran Mexicans learned to cook and from which good cooks spread out into the Mexican countryside. El Charro Café's dining experience reflects the city's long-standing culinary prominence.

❊ ❊ ❊

As her family remembers her, El Charro's founder Monica Flin was a woman larger than life: a flamboyant Auntie Mame who traveled in a sleek black Ford (chauffeured by her brother Stephano, as she never learned to drive) and who always wore a stylish hat. Her pet parrot accompanied her as she greeted customers at the cash register. Monica regularly welcomed a coterie of lady friends to *La Mesa Redonda*, the restaurant's round table, to exchange news and opinions about everything and everyone of significance in Tucson. "Monica loved martinis," Carlotta recalls. "She could not serve them because she didn't have a liquor license. So she made martinis in tall olive jars and boldly poured them from a teapot. Each of the ladies at *La Mesa Redonda* would be given a teacup containing an innocent olive. When they drank their tea, they marveled at the difference an olive can make."

Monica opened the restaurant at a low point in her life. Abandoned by her first husband, a dashing Mexican rancher, then widowed by a second husband, she returned to her hometown of Tucson determined to make good on her own. With rent money borrowed from her sister, she opened El Charro Café, named with what must have been bittersweet memories of her hopes for life in Mexico. *Los Charros* were the proud horsemen of Mexican legend: gallant, skillful, stylish, and romantic. Over the years as the restaurant grew, its décor incorporated the wide-brimmed hats, shiny spurs, bullwhips, and colorful serapes of the rakish Mexican cowboy.

In the beginning, business at the restaurant was far from prosperous. Monica started her venture on what grandniece Carlotta calls *very* short-

El Charro in the late 1930s, or early 1940s

Carlotta Dunn Flores (age 4) and Monica Flin in 1950

term credit. "When a customer arrived to be fed, she would dash out the back door and talk the neighboring Chinese grocer into giving her provisions for the meal. She would then rush back to her kitchen, prepare the meal, serve it, collect her dues, and return to the grocer to pay her bill." At the time, dinner cost fifteen cents.

El Charro changed location three times, eventually coming to the old family home that Monica's father had built in the neighborhood once known as Snob Hollow, just outside the early Spanish *Presidio*. By the time she moved to the current location, Monica and her restaurant had become essential facets of Tucson culture. You could count on an El Charro float in the grand parade for the annual *Fiesta de los Vaqueros*, and when movie production companies came to shoot westerns at Old Tucson (a frontier-town set), the Hollywood cowboys and cowgirls made El Charro their place for good times. It is said that John Wayne used to play cards and have martinis with Monica and that young Ronald Reagan was a fan of her cooking. Politician Thomas Dewey was a visitor, too, but he had no more success at El Charro than he did running for president in 1948. During the campaign, he sat down, unthinkingly picked up a broad flour tortilla and tucked it in his shirt collar, thinking it was a napkin.

When the time came for Monica to retire, she turned over the restaurant to her niece Zarina. "El Charro has always been passed woman to woman," Zarina notes. At the time, Zarina's daughter Carlotta and her husband Ray Flores were living in California. "We came back to Tucson to get the old building ready to sell," Carlotta remembers. "But I took one look at it and remembered all that it had meant to me, to Monica, and to so many people in Tucson, and I said to Ray, 'We cannot sell it!'"

When Carlotta and Ray Flores stepped in, El Charro had a grand reputation, but it was old. They considered it their duty to transform it from a culinary landmark into a dining destination, to make it modern and comfortable. Building on Monica's flamboyant visual theme, they covered the walls with even more pictures of the

Virgin of Guadalupe and the macho gear and outfits of *Los Charros* and began to use Monica's famous Aztec-themed calendars as decor. And they changed the menu—subtly, but with a certainty of purpose far ahead of its time.

"My dad was Mexican and Irish," Carlotta recalls. "He had to have his beer and he had to have his refried beans at every meal. Even at Thanksgiving, there were beans on the side of his turkey." When her father had a heart attack, doctors prescribed a diet for him that Carlotta recalls as nothing but "boiled, mushy, horrible things: canned asparagus and asparagus water." Feeling sorry for him, she began to wonder if there wasn't a better way. That was her inspiration to begin evolving a Mexican cuisine in El Charro's kitchen that is heart-healthy but every bit as tasty and satisfying as its lard-laden counterpart. "Now fitness fare is our way of life," she says. "Even items on the menu that don't seem like they are diet food are good for you, and you'd never even know it. Chile sauce is made without oil; the *almendrado* (Mexican custard) is cholesterol-free. I believe it is possible to eat ethnic foods that are part of your culture and that also taste good and are fun to cook. No one ever need be stuck with two lettuce leaves for dinner just because they want to eat low-fat."

The oldest family-run Mexican restaurant in the U.S. has a new generation to guide it into the twenty-first century—eighty years that make it a virtual miracle of longevity in the mercurial restaurant business. Candace Flores, daughter of Ray and Carlotta, says that although she was not actually born at El Charro, "My mother stopped here on the way home from the hospital. Before going home, she had to come here, because everyone here had to see the new baby." Next door to the café in a space that was once a tortilla factory is Bar *¡Toma!* (*toma* means to drink), a lively Tucson watering hole that is one of many El Charro-related projects undertaken by Raymon Flores, co-author of the book *The Original Guide to Margaritas and Tequila*. Candace, Ray, and Marques, the Flores's three children, are omnipresent at the restaurant, which for them is as much about their family and their hometown as it is about serving good food.

"When people return to Tucson, even after many years away, they come to El Charro because this is the place that represents home to them," Raymon said to us one day. "Sometimes when I look over the dining room and it is filled with people from all over the city, as well as visitors and tourists from the world, I feel as if we do not really own El Charro. It is more like a restaurant that belongs to Tucson. Generations who have lived in this town feel that it is theirs; it is part of who we are; it is a community restaurant that stands for family and tradition. It is the job of my family to open the door and to keep it on course; if we do, it will continue on its own."

What Is a Charro?

✵

"THE IDEA OF THE CHARRO pushes the image of the cowboy to the furthest extreme," explains Raymon Flores, who says that the first thing most newcomers want to know is why the restaurant is named El Charro. In one way, the answer is simple. The charro is an expert horseman. But like those other exemplary equestrians of the New World, the Argentine gaucho and the Texas cowboy, the Mexican charro is an idealized figure whose image gleams with traits of personal honor and national pride. Originally based on the harsh reality of ranch life, the concept of the charro has been dramatically embroidered and transformed into a legend over the years in folk tales, movies, costumes, and music.

The original charros of the early eighteenth century were rugged ranch hands who competed in the *charreada* (rodeo). With a name derived from the Spanish word *charrería* (horsemanship), they were men who came to the ranch festivals to prove their skills and, in doing so, elevate their status above that of mere ranch hand. When they did so, they donned an outfit that broadcast their achievements by mirroring the clothes of the wealthy landowner as brilliantly as possible. In a cultural one-upmanship, the charros showed up their bosses, not only in their equestrian skills, but by the way they dressed in flamboyant outfits studded with silver. Athletic contest, horsemanship demonstration, and cultural celebration, *charrería* came to embody a great sense of national community and pride.

The charros' reputation for bravery and fearlessness extended outside the arena when they were hired by some of the great estates as private militia. Their demeanor was so attractive that by the late nineteenth century, even Mexican bandits were taking on the charro look. Known as *plateados* (the silvered ones), gangs of marauders roamed the countryside trying to look as flashy and act as brave as the real charros. Their horsemanship might have been lacking, but at least they looked the part.

To catch the bandits, the government formed a mounted police force with riders who also dressed in the outfits of the charros. By then it almost didn't matter how good a horseman the rider was; his charro outfit itself came to signify a man who is a

horseman with fine hands, a fighter with mighty fists, a lover, and a Robin-Hood defender of the weak and poor.

When the National Association of Charros was founded on July 4, 1921, the group established standards for the charro look and codified charro behavior. The original manifesto frowned on those who wore bright colors such as yellow, purple, or pink. Such hues were considered unmanly against the *colores serios*, the darker and more somber tones considered appropriate for a man of serious purpose. But even dressed in black, a charro can hardly be missed, for his costume includes a frenzy of embroidery and gleaming silver.

The short tight charro jacket ends at the bottom of the rib cage, sleeves cut short to show off silver wrist cuffs and the ruffled shirt beneath. The jacket is adorned with up to seventy silver (or occasionally gold) buttons, running up the lapels and down the sleeves. The more precious metal a charro flaunts, the higher his status. He wears an enormous sombrero and tight pants with buttons running down the outside of the legs. Traditionally a charro also carried a sidearm. Such an outfit, like that of a matador, is not an easy fashion statement to make. The man who wears it must be slim and graceful and be of demeanor grave enough that he doesn't just look plain silly in his over-the-top attire.

By the 1930s, the charro look had become so popular in Mexico that it was adopted as the official outfit worn by mariachi musicians. Virtually all singing Mexican movie cowboys dressed as charros, and with this adoption of the charro by the world of popular culture, the costume grew even more colorful and elaborate.

Today you can buy a charro costume on the Internet. Type in the word *charro* on your search engine, and you are rewarded with a wealth of embroidered and silvered outfits: classic costumes for men, as well as female variants for lady *charras*, in which the tight pants are replaced by an embroidered floor length skirt. No longer do somber colors rule. They are available, but the catalogues also contain a panoply of intense turquoise, pink, and yellow. They're not inexpensive, but a good charro costume is a once-in-a-lifetime purchase suitable for attending Tucson's annual Fiesta de los Vaqueros or the Charro Days fiesta that has been held every February in Brownsville, Texas, since 1938.

To tradition-minded Mexicans, *charrería* is far more than a sport or a fashion statement. It is a belief system. The charro has come to embody respect for oneself, one's family, and one's fellows, as well as devotion to the highest principles of social justice. This shining ideal crystallized around the time of the Mexican revolution of 1910, when those common men who took up arms against the wealthy landowners were seen as gallant knights—if not in shining armor, then in the garb of the caballero that was bedecked, embroidered, and brilliantly colored. Since that time, charros have been celebrated as descendants of Mexico's freedom fighters—folk heroes who took back Mexico for its people.

Politics, history, and personal pride intertwine in the enduring image of the charro. In his book *Disorder and Progress: Bandits, Police, and Mexican Development*, author Paul Vanderwood writes that the garb of the charro was a way of telling the world that "its wearer could outride,

Ray Flores Sr. with Ray Jr. (age 4) and Marques (age 3)

outrope, outshoot, outdrink, and outwomanize any cowboy from whatever land. "*Yo Soy Mexicano*," a popular song by Jorge Negrete, one of pop culture's premier charros, includes this descriptive verse:

> *Tu orgullo es el charro,*
> *Valiente y bragado.*
> *Traer mi sombrero de plata bordado,*
> *Que nadie me diga que soy un rajado,*
> *Corer mi caballo en pelo montado;*
> *Pero más de todo ser enamorado.*
>
> [Your pride is the charro,
> Valiant and brave.

3

To wear my silver-trimmed hat,
That no one can tell me to back down,
To gallop my horse bareback;
But above all, to be a lover.]

"What the bullfighter is to Spain and the cowboy is to the United States, the charro is to Mexico—a national symbol," writes Kathleen Mullen Sands in the preface to her *Charrería Mexicana*. "Charrería provides an articulation of ethnic pride in Mexico and a mechanism for ethnic identity maintenance in Mexican-American enclaves in the United States."

The charro's combination of horsemanship, derring-do, chivalry, noble purpose, and spectacular wardrobe is expressed throughout El Charro Café—in the art on the calendars, in wall displays of rakish sombreros, and by such essential gear as bullwhips, spurs, embroidered coats, silver bits, and bridles.

No one knows precisely why Monica Flin named her place El Charro, but we can surmise that the unhappy end of her first marriage to a dashing Mexican rancher left her with longings for the quixotic lifestyle—and the handsome caballero—that eluded her. Throughout her reign at the restaurant, and especially in the hands of her progeny, the image of the proud charro defined not only the look of the restaurant, but its style of food, service, and menu. No meal at El Charro is drab or colorless. Every plate that comes from the kitchen has a look that is bold, colorful, and exotic—well suited for the table of a valiant caballero.

"To me, the charro represents a vital side of Tucson culture," Raymon Flores Jr. says. "It is all about embellishment, drama, and excitement, as well as the honor of our ancestors. That is the spirit that infuses this restaurant. The charro is our way of life."

Popular culture's best-known charros have combined singing and acting with the athletic prowess of *charrería*. They include Pedro Infante, a one-time carpenter who became a matinee idol until he died in a plane crash in 1957; Jorge Negrete, a mellifluous baritone who was actually related to Miguel Negrete, Don Pedro María Anaya, and Pedro Moreno, all true heroes of the War for Mexican Independence; and the living-legend Antonio Aguilar, a truly gifted horseman, star of 150 movies, and singer of dozens of chart-topping charro songs known simply as the *Charro of Mexico*. Even Elvis Presley took his crack at the image in his 1969 movie ¡*Charro!*—a rare break from his usual happy-go-lucky movie roles in that he went through the picture unshaven and sullen and sang only once, the title song, ¡*Charro!*

Breakfast

(Desayuno)

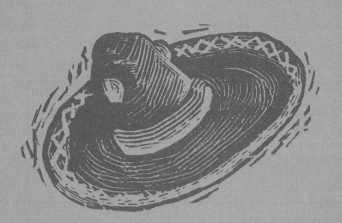

MOST AMERICANS who didn't grow up eating Mexican food think of it as lunch or supper. But Tucsonians eat three meals a day; and the grains that play such an important part in their cookery are the basis of some terrific breakfasts. Indeed, if all you're having is *huevos rancheros,* which is basically eggs with salsa, there's no breadstuff better for mopping up a runny yolk than a torn-off piece of a tortilla; and a mild-flavored, steaming-hot tamale, with or without an egg alongside, can be a good morning meal. El Charro doesn't open early for breakfast, but Sunday brunch is a popular meal, when the menu includes eggs scrambled with spicy *chorizo* (sausage) accompanied by *frijoles refritos* (refried beans) and warm tortillas.

Good Morning Tucson Burrito

Breakfast burritos have become popular across the country since everyone is discovering how versatile a tortilla can be. The recipe below can be modified to your personal taste by substituting bacon, ham, *chorizo* (sausage), other cheeses, or by adding scallions or mushrooms. The potatoes can be made quickly, or even better, if they are leftovers from the evening meal—add them.

3	*eggs*
1	*cup grated Cheddar cheese*
	Flour tortillas (use the larger ones for better wrapping)
1	*cup roasted, red skin potatoes, diced*
1	*cup chopped ham (or substitute bacon, chorizo, turkey)*
	Salt and pepper
	Your favorite salsa

Scramble the eggs. Place a thin layer of cheese on the tortillas, and add the warm eggs, potatoes, and meat (and scallions and mushrooms if you like the Dagwood approach to burrito making). Season to taste with salt and pepper. Heat for 2 minutes in a warm oven (just enough to melt the cheese, not to dry out the tortillas.) Have salsa on hand for an added touch of spice to start your day.

MAKES 4 TO 6 SERVINGS

Chiliquiles
Layered Egg and Cheese Casserole

This breakfast treat will be familiar to anyone who has ever done a 7-layer casserole. This is easy to make, and will add a southwestern touch to any buffet or brunch.

	Corn tortilla chips
3	to 4 eggs, scrambled
1	cup Cheddar cheese, grated
	Enchilada Sauce (page 90)
1	cup chopped green onion
1	cup frozen (or canned) corn
1	(6 to 7-ounce) can of diced hot green chiles

Preheat the oven to 350°F (175°C). Layer the ingredients in this order: the corn chips, eggs, cheese, enchilada sauce, green onion, corn, and chiles. Bake for 20 minutes.

MAKES 3 TO 4 SERVINGS

Spiced Zucchini Muffins

Like carrot cake, zucchini muffins are a delectable sweet that have the cache of good health because they include vegetables. We like Carlotta's spiced zucchini muffins as a coffee companion in the morning.

3	eggs
½	cup oil
1	cup sugar
½	cup sour cream
1½	cups grated zucchini (any zucchini in season)
1½	cups all-purpose flour
½	cup whole wheat flour
2	teaspoons baking powder
1	teaspoon baking soda
¼	teaspoon salt
1½	teaspoons cinnamon (use fresh whenever possible)
¼	teaspoon nutmeg
¼	teaspoon ground cloves
1	cup dried fruit—raisins, cranberries, cherries (optional)
½	cup chopped walnuts (optional)

Preheat the oven to 350°F (175°C). Grease and paper muffin tins. Mix the eggs, oil, sugar, sour cream, and zucchini together in a large bowl. Do not overmix. Add the two flours, baking powder, baking soda, salt, cinnamon, nutmeg, cloves, and fruit and walnuts, if using. (I like to sift my dry ingredients together to blend them.) Do not overmix, but make sure that all the batter is mixed together. Pour into the muffin tins, and bake for approximately 20 minutes.

MAKES 7 TEXAS-SIZED (8 TO 10 REGULAR-SIZED) MUFFINS

Carmen Miranda's Morning Glory Special

Since Monica Flin was quite the connoisseur of hats, we thought she would appreciate this recipe, which was named in honor of Carmen Miranda's spectacular choice in hats.

4	eggs
1¼	cups oil
2	cups sugar
2	teaspoons vanilla
2	cups flour
2	teaspoons baking powder
1	teaspoon baking soda
¼	teaspoon salt
2½	teaspoons cinnamon
2½	cups grated carrots
2	cups crushed pineapple, drained
½	cup shredded coconut
½	cup raisins
1	cup chopped walnuts

Preheat the oven to 350°F (175°C). Grease your muffin tins. Mix together the eggs, oil, sugar, and vanilla. Do not overmix. Sift the flour, baking powder, baking soda, salt, and cinnamon, into the mixture.

Fold the carrots, pineapple, coconut, raisins, and walnuts into the batter. Pour into the greased muffin tins, and bake for approximately 20 minutes. For an extra bit of flavor, grate fresh cinnamon over the muffins when you first take them out of the oven.

MAKES 8 TEXAS-SIZED MUFFINS

Appetizers

(Aperitivos)

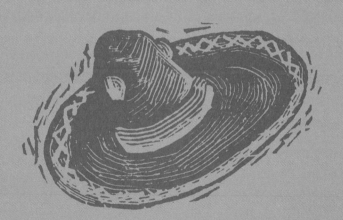

IT IS INCONCEIVABLE to start a meal at El Charro without a *Tostada Grande*, the crisp flour tortilla that can be served simply warm with a little butter melted on top or crowned with more toppings than a round-the-world pizza. The beauty of a *Tostada Grande* is its fragile crispness, even when it is blanketed with melted cheese, carne seca, and/or guacamole. Carlotta notes that the secret of its crispness is to bake the tortilla at 400 degrees for a few minutes before adding toppings. If the tortilla is a little dry, it should be spread with a thin film of margarine or butter before baking.

Guacamole
Avocado Dip

Contrary to culinary mythology, there really is no way to keep guacamole from turning brown. Make guacamole as close to serving time as possible. Serve in a lettuce cup, topped with red bell pepper strips.

4	large avocados, seeded, peeled, and mashed
4	large tomatoes, diced
½	cup fresh Anaheim chiles, roasted (page 79) chopped
1½	teaspoons garlic salt
	Pinch of dried oregano
¼	cup white onion, chopped
1	cup shredded longhorn cheese or other cheese

In a large mixing bowl combine the avocados, tomatoes, chiles, garlic salt, oregano, onion, and cheese, mixing well. Cover the bowl with plastic wrap and refrigerate until ready to serve. Serve with *totopos* (corn chips, page 113), or use as filling for a vegetarian Burro.

MAKES ABOUT 5 CUPS

Quesadilla
Mexican Grilled Cheese Sandwich

To Mexicans, "Queso quesadilla" is a mild, white, raw-milk cheese that turns creamy when it melts. To Americans, the term quesadilla means cheese melted into a folded-over tortilla, creating a slim version of the grilled cheese sandwich. It is also possible to make iconoclastic quesadillas using corn tortillas rather than flour tortillas. The result, Carlotta notes, "is a totally different taste and appearance . . . with higher nutritional value and only a trace of fat." This is the favorite way of Zarina Flores, Carlotta's mother, who likes small corn tortillas with just a "smattering of Mexican white cheese, grilled to tasty perfection."

16	to 32 ounces panela or nonfat cheese, crumbled
12	(10-inch) flour tortillas
	Oil or vegetable spray

OPTIONAL FILLINGS:

Fresh Anaheim or Jalapeño chiles, roasted (page 79)

Diced chicken or beef, cooked and shredded

Divide the cheese and optional fillings into 12 portions. Place one portion in the center of the first tortilla. Fold the tortilla in half and flatten it gently. Secure it with a wooden pick if necessary. Repeat with the remaining tortillas. Lightly oil, or spray with vegetable oil, a large skillet. Place the skillet over medium heat for 2 minutes; then place the prepared tortillas on the hot skillet and cook for about 1 minute. Carefully flip the tortilla and cook the other side until brown. Serve immediately. For easier handling, cut into wedges.

MAKES 1 DOZEN

Los Chachos
Corn Tortilla Chips with Melted Cheese

The very fact that nachos are included in this book, even if called *Los Chachos* to honor the name El Charro, roils Ray Flores Sr. "Ball park food!" he calls them with disdain. Nachos are NOT traditionally Tucsonan, nor are they true Mexican. They are, perhaps, Tex-Mex; or more truthfully, gringo-Mex, as they are infinitely more popular throughout the U.S. than they are south of the border. Nevertheless, enough people who eat in Mexican restaurants *expect* to begin their meal with nachos that they have indeed found a place on the El Charro menu.

4	cups totopos (corn chips, page 113)
16	ounces longhorn cheese, shredded
6	fresh Anaheim chiles, roasted (page 79) chopped
3	large tomatoes, chopped

GARNISH:

1	cup green olives, chopped
1	cup avocado chunks
	Jalapeño rings
	Chopped onions or scallions
	Diced red or green bell pepper
	Sour cream
	Refried beans

Preheat the oven to 400°F (205°C). Arrange the chips, overlapping slightly, on a pizza pan or cookie sheet. Sprinkle evenly with the cheese, chile, and tomatoes. Bake for 5 minutes, or until the cheese melts. Garnish as desired before serving.

[Notita: The microwave speeds up the process, but does not develop flavors as well as baking in a conventional oven.]

MAKES 6 TO 8 SERVINGS

Super Bowl Fundido con Sabores de Chiles
Cheese Fondue with Chiles

Fondue, or *fundido*, means a hot or melted food, usually cheese or chocolate, often with wine or liqueur added. Dip chips, cubes of cake or French bread, vegetable sticks, or bite-size pieces of fruit into the hot mixture. This version is especially good to serve when the whole family gets together at home to watch a big event like the Super Bowl.

½	pound feta-and-garlic cheese, crumbled
½	pound processed Jack-and-green chile cheese, grated
½	pound longhorn cheese, grated
½	pound Mexican cheese, grated
2	jalapeños, sliced into rings
1	chipotle chile, sliced into rings
1	fresh Anaheim chile, roasted (page 79) cut into rings
6	tablespoons Taco Sauce (page 88) or other salsa
	Chips
½	cup chopped onion

Prepare a microwaveable casserole dish with vegetable oil spray. Sprinkle the cheeses in an even layer. Mix all the chiles together and sprinkle them on top, along with the taco sauce or salsa. Microwave on high until bubbly. Serve with your favorite chips, chopped onion, and more salsa.

[Notita: Pour the melted cheese mixture over individual servings of chips and top with chiles for a deluxe version of ballpark nachos.]

MAKES 6 TO 8 SERVINGS

Tostada Grande de Tucson
Original Large Cheese Crisp

You cannot make a tostada grande without a flour tortilla that is itself truly grand. Outside of Tucson, eighteen-inch tortillas can be hard to come by, so it is possible to make a tostada *pequeño* (small) using the same principle. At El Charro, the big tortillas are cut into triangles and served on silver pedestals so all at the table easily can grab a piece. In Tucson homes it is traditional for each person to present the tostada grande whole. Everybody tears off a *bocadito* (little mouthful) and spoons on a bit of salsa picante.

The beauty of the basic tostada is that the cheese is melted tightly to the tortilla, so nothing falls off when you hoist a piece. Add other ingredients at the risk of spillage!

1	(18-inch) flour tortilla
16	ounces longhorn cheese, shredded

Preheat the oven to 400°F (205°C). Bake the tortilla for 5 minutes directly on the rack in the oven. Remove the tortilla from the oven and place it on a pizza pan. Spread the cheese evenly over the tortilla and bake until the cheese is bubbly and completely melted, about 5 minutes. Serve the tortilla on a pizza tray or other round platter.

MAKES 4 TO 8 APPETIZER SERVINGS

Breads
(Pan)
Tortillas & Tamales

MY CHILDHOOD WAS FILLED with the sweet smell of *masa*," Carlotta writes, referring to the dough made from ground dried corn or wheat flour. Corn *masa (masa de elote)* is the most fragrant kind, used for rolling out tortillas. In some of Tucson's top Mexican restaurants, when you order a taco, the tortilla for that taco is made fresh from a large bowl of *masa*. The corn meal is flattened out in a tortilla press, then griddle-cooked until its hot corn aroma billows up all around and it attains a light, velvety texture.

Carlotta's Calabaza Pan
Pumpkin Bread

Pumpkin bread is a *pan dulce* (sweet bread) that is served with coffee at breakfast. It makes a nice snack any time of day or night.

2	cups canned pumpkin
4	eggs
2	cups sugar (pilonelle, or cone sugar, if possible)
1	cup oil
3⅓	cups flour
2	teaspoons baking soda
3½	teaspoons baking powder
1½	teaspoons salt
1	teaspoon cinnamon (whenever possible, use fresh or grated cinnamon for better flavor)
1	teaspoon nutmeg
1	cup chopped walnuts (optional)
1	cup raisins (optional)

Preheat the oven to 350°F (175°C). Grease two 8 x 4-inch pans. Whisk the pumpkin, eggs, sugar, and oil together. Do not over mix. Add the flour, baking soda, baking powder, salt, cinnamon, nutmeg, and walnuts and raisins, if using, to the mixture. Mix until evenly blended. Pour the mixture into the pans, and bake for approximately 40 minutes. Use a toothpick to test the center. When the pick comes out clean but moist, the bread is done.

[Notita: While it may be tempting to use old Halloween pumpkins for your baking, don't bother. The canned pumpkin is much easier to work with and much tastier.]

MAKES 2 (8 X 4-INCH) LOAVES

Pan de Elote
Cornbread

No matter where you are from, everyone has a recipe for cornbread. Our recipe incorporates chiles and jalapeños, and can involve nuts, dried fruit, and herbs if you want to experiment. The basic recipe is as follows, but don't be afraid to try something new—cornbread is a very forgiving bread.

1	cup yellow cornmeal
1	cup flour
1	cup sugar
1	tablespoon baking powder
⅓	teaspoon salt
¾	cup milk (or buttermilk)
½	cup sour cream
2	eggs
6	tablespoons melted butter
1	small can diced chiles or jalapeños, drained
1	small can white kernel baby corn, drained

Mix together the cornmeal, flour, sugar, baking powder, and salt. Add the milk, sour cream, and eggs, and blend together. Add the melted butter, chiles, and baby corn. For extra crunch, try adding pine nuts or dried fruit such as cranberries. Preheat the oven to 350°F (175°C). Grease the pan. Just before you are ready to pour the mixture into the pan, briefly heat the pan in oven. The hot oil forms a pleasant crust for your bread. Don't let the oil smoke. (To test, just sprinkle water; it should sizzle.) You can use a bread pan, a square 9 x 9-inch pan, or, for truly traditional cornbread, use an iron skillet.

MAKES 12 TO 15 SERVINGS

Enchiladas Sonorenses
Flat Corn Masa Patties with Red Chile Sauce

This is the basic masa shell, wonderful with a little sauce, cheese, and cabbage or lettuce. Like tacos or tostadas, it can carry any of the beef, pork, poultry, fish, or vegetable fillings offered elsewhere in this book.

2	pounds fresh corn masa
1	teaspoon salt
½	teaspoon baking soda
1	medium potato, cooked and grated (for fluffiness)
½	cup shredded Cheddar cheese
	Oil for frying

GARNISH:

4	cups Enchilada Sauce (page 90)
1	cup sliced green olives
1	cup chopped green onions
1	cup shredded longhorn cheese, or other cheese
	Sliced radish
	Lime slice
1	ounce vinegar
1	tablespoon dried oregano
1	or 2 heads iceberg lettuce (or 1 head green cabbage), shredded

Mix the masa, salt, soda, potato, and cheese. Shape into balls the size of an egg. Place the balls, one at a time, between two sheets of wax paper, and flatten them with a rolling pin or tortilla press to 4 or 5 inches in diameter, or ¼ inch thick, whichever you arrive at first. Make these ahead and cover with damp paper towels. Heat 1 inch of oil in a small skillet, fry each patty 5 minutes on each side, and drain on paper towels.

To garnish: Cover each patty with hot Enchilada Sauce, and top with the olives, onions, cheese, radish, and lime. Mix the vinegar and dried oregano in a small bowl, and serve on the side with a bowl of the shredded lettuce or cabbage.

MAKES 6 TO 8 SERVINGS

Tamales

The ultimate comfort food" is how Carlotta Flores describes the tamale. "To our family and our extended family, it is our history and tradition—not just meat and masa—that are wrapped in tamales. I recall the comfort of tamales at times of bereavement, at times of joy, at times of closeness with others. This ancient food holds memories good and sad—but most of all, it contains our family identity."

At Christmas El Charro hosts its own version of the time-honored *tamalada*, a tamale party, at which expert cooks demonstrate how to make the simple but exacting dish that is so essential to Mexican cookery. The varieties they make are far flung, from *tamales de chile Colorado* (the classic red tamale) to the yuletide sweet bean tamale made with raisins, brown sugar, and cinnamon to pumpkin/cranberry tamales, even tofu tamales. Carlotta has identified fifty different kinds of tamale, the two basic kinds being the regular tamale made in a dried corn husk that must be softened in warm water before shaping, and the green tamale of late summer and early fall (corn season) that is made in fresh, soft husks that impart an earthier flavor to the masa inside.

Tamales are as essential to Christmas in the Mexican house as cookies are in other cultures. It is traditional for families to gather on Christmas Eve to make and eat tamales. The best way to learn to make a tamale is to watch someone do it (hence El Charro's demonstrations every Christmas) because while it is a simple process, it requires a significant amount of work. As Carlotta says, it is "not something to attempt if there is anything else you would rather be doing." She does offer these basic tips to lead the tamale maker on the right path:

Never cook tamales in an aluminum pot or steam them under aluminum foil. If your pot does not have a good lid and you must use aluminum foil, first place white freezer paper over the tamales, then layer on the foil to form a seal on the steamer. If the tamales are ever close to aluminum, you will taste it!

If making green corn tamales, use the corn the day it is ground. Fresh corn does not retain its sweet flavor longer than a day.

While red tamales may be frozen without harm, green tamales change for the worse in the freezer and take on "a hint of sourness." Red tamales reheat well in the microwave oven wrapped in damp paper towels. If making red tamales, the meat mixture can be prepared a day or two in advance, thus cutting down on the workload of tamale-making day.

Consider the tamale a breakfast food. Leave the steamed tamale in its husk and heat it in the oven until the husk turns crisp. Open the husk and top the hot steamy corn with a fried egg.

Tamales de Chile Colorado
Red Chile Tamales

Don't let the length of this recipe discourage you," Carlotta advises. Tamale-making, while time-consuming, is not difficult. And it is a great occasion for a cooking party among friends and family. "Every family I know has a story unique to its tamales," Carlotta says. "As families divide and scatter, these recipes have traveled with them."

MEAT MIXTURE:

3	pounds roast beef (brisket)
3	pounds roast fresh pork (butt)
3	quarts water
¼	cup garlic purée (page 93)
1	tablespoon salt

SAUCE:

2	quarts water
1	pound dried red chiles
¾	cup vegetable shortening
¾	cup flour
6	cups reserved beef/pork broth

MASA DOUGH:

2	(30-count) packages dried corn husks
1¼	pounds vegetable shortening
5	pounds corn masa
3	teaspoons salt
2	cups reserved beef/pork broth
¼	cup red chile purée (for instructions, see below)
	Green olives, with pits

DAY ONE

In a 10-quart stockpot, bring the meats and water to a boil. Skim off the froth. Add the garlic purée and salt. Reduce the heat, and simmer until the meats are tender, skimming frequently. Remove the meats; strain and reserve the broth, storing it in the refrigerator. Shred the meats, removing all the fat, bone, and gristle. Cover and refrigerate. When the broth is chilled, remove and discard the fat.

Sauce

Remove the stems from the chiles, and place the pods in a pot with the water. Bring them to a boil, and simmer until the pods soften. Strain and reserve the broth. In a blender, process the chiles a few at a time with a little broth until smooth. In a 10-quart stockpot, melt the vegetable shortening. Whisk in the flour to make a golden brown roux. Heat the reserved broth, and slowly whisk it into the roux. Add the chile purée, and simmer for 20 minutes. Stir the shredded, cooked meats into the sauce, and simmer to blend the seasonings. Taste, and correct the seasonings. Store in the refrigerator.

[Notita: Can be prepared a day or two ahead up to this point.]

DAY TWO

First, soften the corn husks in hot water for 10 minutes. Remove the silks, and clean the husks. Drain, and cover with a damp towel. To make the masa dough, beat the vegetable shortening in small batches until very light and fluffy—the consistency of whipped cream. Place half the vegetable shortening in an electric mixer. Beat for at least 10 minutes until very soft and fluffy. Meanwhile bring 2 cups of the reserved broth to a simmer. When the vegetable shortening is fully beaten, add half the masa and the simmering broth a spoonful at a time, beating constantly. Add half the salt, and, if desired, fold in ¼ cup of chile purée for color. Remove to a large bowl. Repeat with the remaining ingredients.

[Notita: To test the masa dough to see if it is fluffy enough, drop a pinch of dough into a glass of cold water. It is perfect if it floats.]

To assemble:

Open a large corn husk with the pointed end at the bottom. Spread 2 tablespoons masa dough onto the husk to within 1 inch of its edges. Place 1 heaping tablespoon of meat filling and an olive in the center of the masa dough. Tightly roll the corn husk lengthwise around the filling. Fold the pointed end up. Repeat with the remaining masa dough and filling. Place the tamales, open end up, in the refrigerator or freezer 1 to 2 hours before steaming.

To steam, place the tamales on a rock in a steamer (or improvise a steamer by resting a wire rack on clean stones, empty tuna cans, or corn cobs in a Dutch oven or large kettle). Add water to just below the rack. Arrange the tamales, open end up, on the rack. Bring the water to a boil; cover, reduce the heat, and steam for about 45 minutes. Add boiling water as necessary, but be sure the tamales do not sit in the water.

[Notita: Red tamales reheat well in the microwave oven wrapped in damp paper towels, or in a conventional oven, wrapped in foil.]

[Notita: Tamales make a wonderful breakfast dish. Leave the steamed tamale in its husk, and heat it in the oven until the husk is crispy. Open the husk, and top with a fried egg.]

MAKES 5 DOZEN

Tamales de Elote
Green Corn Tamales

Green corns are here!" is a sign posted annually in El Charro's window late in the summer. That means that sweet corn is at its peak and green corn tamales are on the menu. Made from fresh, sweet corn (that is actually white in color), the green corn tamales range from simple sweet-corn mush in fresh husks to corn mixed with cheese and chiles.

5	dozen ears fresh white (green) corn
2½	pounds vegetable shortening
2	tablespoons salt
2	tablespoons sugar
2	pounds longhorn or Mexican cheese, shredded
2	cups cottage cheese
4	cups fresh Anaheim chiles, roasted (page 79) chopped

GARNISH:

2	cups salsa

Husk, rinse, and drain the corn. Scrape the kernels from the cob with a knife. Be careful not to cut into the cob. Grind the corn in a blender or meat grinder. Immediately after grinding the kernels, use an electric mixer to whip the vegetable shortening and salt, in batches, until fluffy. Combine the beaten shortening mixture and ground corn to form green-corn masa. In another large bowl, combine the sugar, cheese, cottage cheese, and chiles.

To make the tamales, the masa should be thick. Select the biggest husks for the tamales. Place 2 tablespoons of the masa in the center of one husk. Now place a table-spoonful of the cheese-and-chile mixture in the center of the masa. Fold the left edge of the corn husk over to the right edge of the filling. Fold the right edge over the left. Fold up the bottom third of the husk, and turn the tamale over to keep it intact. Place the open end up in a pan. Repeat until the filling is used up. Refrigerate or freeze to congeal and then wrap. Steam the tamales according to the directions for Red Chile Tamales (page 26), and serve with salsa on the side.

MAKES 5 DOZEN

Flour Tortillas

The huge flour tortilla is Tucson's daily bread. By *huge*, we mean a full eighteen inches in diameter—that's standard size in local tortilla factories—and by *daily bread*, we mean that it is a food eaten morning, noon, and night. It is a wrap for a breakfast burro or a suppertime chimichanga; it is served folded in quarters alongside meals so you can tear off a little piece (a *bocadito*, meaning "little mouthful") and use it to scoop refritos off your plate or dip it in the yolks of *huevos rancheros*. And it is served plain and warm, lightly buttered, as a snack any time. Spread out flat and baked in the oven, the flour tortilla becomes the basis for a *tostada grande* a.k.a. Mexican pizza—a crisp, ultrathin circle topped with melted cheese, *carne seca*, guacamole, and/or beans.

Foot-wide flour tortillas are now available in most American supermarkets and tortilla-making machines are growing nearly as common as brick ovens, but Tucson remains the best place to eat flour tortillas. And it isn't only their size that makes them special. To walk into a tortilla bakery in a Mexican neighborhood and smell the heady fresh-cooked aroma is to know why Tucsonans consider this simple bread their staff of life. Thin as it is, a flour tortilla has body and soul, and real earthy flavor. It is sturdy enough to hold a boatload of ingredients, yet so fine-textured that it is a pleasure to eat absolutely plain.

Carlotta Flores explains that Tucson took to the flour tortilla because wheat thrived in the mild winters. Farmers found that they could grow two crops a year. "So while elsewhere in the New World corn remained king, Tucson became the hometown of the 'flour' tortilla." Carlotta notes that as farming methods improved, corn regained its place in the Tucson diet. Now corn tortillas are popular as well, but Tucson's passion for the giant flour tortilla remains strong.

Ray Flores Sr. believes it is getting harder to find a really good flour tortilla, and in Tucson, that's a serious problem. "There is something about the old families," he says. "They had the right touch, the right feel to stretch the dough. It's not something you learn to do overnight. And the good old tortilla makers are passing on."

Ray recalls that long ago when he was a child growing up in Tucson, he and his father used to go to the kitchen of some ladies who made wonderful tortillas. "They were small ones, only fourteen to sixteen inches wide, but there was something different about them," he says. "They weren't as white, and they had such flavor! One day my dad and I watched what they did. They mixed the dough by hand, and they wet their hands a little as they mixed. They *felt* the dough every step of the way—something you could not do if you used a mixer. We bought those tortillas by the dozen and used them for every meal. One day the ladies went out of business, and I've looked for them ever since."

Ray believes that even very good corn tortillas aren't all that interesting. "Most of them get fried anyway," he says. "So it doesn't really matter what they taste like. One of his pet peeves is the automatic association so many people make between nachos (made with corn tortilla chips) and Mexican food. "A man came into El Charro one day and wanted to know if we served nachos," he snorts. 'No,' I said. 'What do you think this is, a ball park?' In fact, as part of its policy to offer a broad range of choices to dinner guests, nachos have been added to the menu—much to Ray's chagrin.

Here are the basic uses for tortillas:

FLOUR TORTILLAS
- wrap for a burro (made with eighteen-inch tortillas)
- wrap for a burrito (made with smaller tortillas)
- wrap for a chimichanga, a deep-fried burro, or for a sandwich
- wrap for won-tons or pot stickers
- companion to almost any meal, for mopping, scooping, and dipping in food, generally served folded into quarter circles, and kept warm and moist in a small basket
- breakfast breadstuff, served warm and buttered
- baked crisp, served flat, and topped with cheese, known as a *tostada grande*
- dessert: warmed, buttered, and sprinkled with cinnamon sugar

CORN TORTILLAS
- chips, for dipping, or strips like croutons for soup or salad
- tacos, fried crisp and filled
- tostadas: flat tacos
- enchiladas: soft corn dough either rolled or layered flat (*enchiladas Sonorenses*) with such other ingredients as *carne seca*, vegetables, guacamole, beans, and chili
- gordita: literally, "little fatties," smaller and thicker and used as the foundation for hearty meats such as barbecue
- chalupa: corn dough formed to hold ingredients of choice

Tortillas de Harina
Flour Tortillas

Wrapped snugly, tortillas freeze well. They may be defrosted while still wrapped.

8	cups all-purpose flour
1	tablespoon salt
½	plus ¼ cup lard
2¼	cups warm water

In a large bowl mix together the flour and salt. Using your hands, quickly blend the ½ cup lard into flour mixture. Gradually add the warm water, mixing constantly until a soft dough (not sticky) is obtained. Turn out the dough on a floured board and knead for 10 minutes. Pat it lightly with some of the additional lard, cover with a dish towel, and set aside to rest 5 minutes. Divide the dough into about 24 pieces the size of tennis balls. Pat each ball with lard, cover with waxed paper, and let rest 30 minutes. Shape the dough balls into tortillas (traditionally, the flour tortilla is patted out by hand; however, a rolling pin may be used). Flour the board generously and roll the dough into circles about 6 to 8 inches in diameter—or larger and thinner, if things are going well.

Meanwhile, heat the *comal* (or a large, heavy, well-seasoned griddle) to very hot. (It is hot enough when drops of water on it sizzle instantly.) Do not grease it. Bake the tortillas on the *comal* until they bubble slightly. Flip the tortilla, and cook the other side. Tortillas will characteristically brown in the areas where the dough bubbled and remain white elsewhere. They can be held for a short time before serving wrapped well in foil or plastic. Eat them as soon as possible.

MAKES ABOUT 2 DOZEN

Burros (aka Burritos)

Burro is the Mexican term for a downsized donkey; but in most Mexican kitchens it has come to mean a very large, wrapped-up meal (the plump girth of which resembles a sturdy little equine). Strangely, most Mexican restaurants in the U.S. refer to this substantial tortilla-wrapped package by its diminutive name, burrito, despite the fact that most burritos are huge.

Think of the burro as a concept more than a recipe. Like an omelet, you can fill it however you like. El Charro (which does not even list *burritos* on the menu) serves burros twelve different ways, including the no-meat bean burro and the veggie burro, as well as burros filled with ground beef, carne seca, chicken, and chile.

Vegetarian Burrito

Vegetarians can have a great burrito using their favorite vegetables and pico de gallo or salsa. A favorite at the restaurant includes whole beans (you can use pinto or black beans), rice, mushrooms, and spinach, which can be steamed or used fresh.

6	(12-inch) flour tortillas
1	cup cooked whole or refried beans
1	cup cooked rice
½	cup sliced mushrooms
½	cup choped onion
1	cup shredded Cheddar cheese
1	cup steamed spinach
1	cup chopped tomatoes
1	cup salsa
1	cup sour cream

Lay out 1 flour tortilla on a flat surface. Place about 2 tablespoons of each ingredient into the tortilla, layering together so that you can still roll the tortilla. Roll the tortilla (see page 33) and repeat using all the tortillas and all the ingredients.

[Notita: For your vegetarian friends, grilled vegetables such as onions, peppers, mushrooms will make a tasty burrito. For tofu fans, include chunks of tofu instead of any cheese.]

MAKES 6 BURROS

Grilled Meat Burrito

Today, many cooks enjoy grilling their meats. It is a fast and flavorful way to cook chicken, beef, or shrimp. After marinating your beef or chicken strips (or shrimp) you can make a tasty burrito using your favorite ingredients such as fresh peppers (or try marinated peppers if fresh are not available), onions, mushrooms, cabbage, spinach, avocado, bacon, tomatoes. A tomato based salsa is always a treat but don't be afraid to try a fruit salsa such as mango or pineapple with your burrito.

6	(12-inch) flour tortillas
2	cups grilled chicken (beef or shrimp), shredded
1	cup rice
1	cup cooked whole or refried beans
1	cup cup sliced fresh bell peppers (green or red)
1	cup grilled sliced mushrooms
1	cup choped onion
1	cup chopped tomatoes
1	cup sour cream
1	cup salsa (tomato or fruit)
1	cup shredded Cheddar cheese

Lay out 1 flour tortilla on a flat surface. Place about 2 tablespoons of each ingredient into the tortilla, layering together so that you can still roll the tortilla. Roll the tortilla (see page 33) and repeat using all the tortillas and all the ingredients.

MAKES 6 BURROS

The Great Thingamajig

Chimichanga translates as *thingamajig,* and there can be little doubt when you see one that it is descended from the burro. That, in fact, is what it is: a burro that has been deep fried so that it resembles one gigantic egg roll. While the term *chimi* became popular in Tucson, there is no doubt that many other places had a similar food, but over the years it became best-known as a Tucson dish. Today it is popular in Mexican restaurants everywhere.

Most Tucsonans believe that El Charro invented it. Chicago chef Rick Bayless, of Frontera Grill and author of *Authentic Mexican,* contends the fried packet originated in Baja California, where it was known as a *chivechanga.* On the other hand, folklore has Monica Flin accidentally dropping a stuffed burro into a vat of sizzling oil, then christening the mistake chimichanga. Carlotta says that it is likely the chimichanga was first deep-fried as a way to offset the flavor of the goat meat that was often used as its filling. Whatever the origins of the chimichanga, El Charro definitely serves the best and the biggest. You can get it filled with whatever you like.

To make a chimichanga, use the same rolling technique as for the burro (page 33), filling it with your choice of meat or poultry fillings. Fasten the seam well with wooden picks and deep fry it in a large pot or deep-fryer in 360°F oil until it is golden brown on all sides. Use tongs to remove the browned chimi, and drain it on multiple layers of paper towel. Remove the wooden picks before serving. Provide guests with shredded cheese, avocado slices, lettuce, salsa, and sour cream so they can crack their chimi open and garnish it to their taste.

Soups

(Sopas)

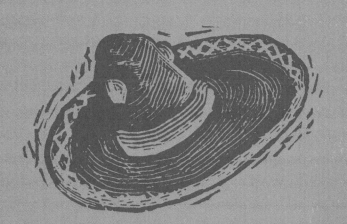

CARLOTTA SAYS, "A delicious soup can cure all ills—heartbreak, a chill, illness, or simple hunger. To be offered a bowl of homemade soup is to be offered a part of someone's soul.

Other than albóndigas, all of El Charro's soups are based on stock that is made by simmering bones and a few vegetables in water with herbs and spices. Start with a big pot of cold water. Add a few pounds of beef and/or chicken bones, bring the water to a boil, and let the bones simmer, uncovered for several hours, with seasonings of choice. As the stock cooks, a froth will form on the top. Use a spoon to skim it off. The longer the stock simmers, the richer its flavor. When cooked to your satisfaction, remove the pot from the heat and let it cool. Discard the bones and strain the stock for use in soups, sauces, rice, or pasta dishes.

Carlotta recommends always to make lots of stock so you can use some immediately and freeze the rest to use for making soups or sauces at a later time.

Albóndigas
Meatball Soup

Albóndigas means "meatball," which Carlotta finds a wholly inadequate word to describe a soup that is, in fact a featherweight appetizer. Albóndigas can be a main course if you serve each person six meatballs instead of three, and if you offer side dishes of refried beans and flour or corn tortillas. "Or, for a change, serve it with French bread," Carlotta suggests. Bread has been "a welcome alternative to tortillas in the Mexican diet ever since the French influence of Emperor Maximilian in the 1860s."

Carlotta also points out that a low-fat version of this soup easily can be made by making the meatballs from ground turkey and substituting egg white or an egg substitute for the egg.

BROTH:		**MEATBALLS:**	
3	quarts water	2	pounds ground chuck, 90%
1	whole white onion		lean
2	ripe tomatoes, minced	½	cup garlic purée, (page 93)
3	green onions, chopped	1	egg
½	cup fresh cilantro (substitute	1	teaspoon salt, or to taste
	fresh parsley or 1 teaspoon	1	teaspoon ground black pepper
	dried coriander)	½	cup flour (or 1 slice wet bread)
2	teaspoons dried oregano	6	to 8 fresh mint leaves, chopped
			(optional)
		¼	cup uncooked rice (optional)

In an 8-quart stockpot, bring the water to the boil. Add the onion. About 15 minutes before the soup is finished, add the tomatoes, green onions, cilantro, and dried oregano. Taste and adjust the seasonings. Meanwhile, in a large bowl, mix the ground chuck with the garlic purée, egg, salt, pepper, flour or bread, and the rice and mint, if desired. Form the mixture into balls the size of walnuts. Carefully add the meatballs to the boiling water, reduce the heat and simmer 30 minutes, skimming off froth frequently. Serve as a first course with three meatballs, or as a main meal with more meatballs.

MAKES 6 TO 8 SERVINGS

1922, The Year El Charro Opens, Is Also the Year in Which . . .

- 3-D movies debut; red & green eyeglasses give depth to the movie *Power of Love*.
- "April Showers" by Al Jolson is the #1 best-selling record.
- A&W opens its first root beer stand in Sacramento, California.
- Annie Oakley sets a trap-shooting record by breaking one hundred clay targets in a row.
- Babe Ruth signs a three-year contract with the New York Yankees.
- Butter, formerly sold in bulk, is first made available in one-pound packages.
- Charles Atlas is declared the World's Most Perfectly Developed Man.
- Coca-Cola's advertising theme for 1922 is Thirst Knows No Season.
- Country Club Plaza—America's first shopping center—opens in Kansas City.
- Emily Post publishes the first edition of *Etiquette*.
- Eskimo Pie ice cream treat is patented (in Iowa).
- F. Scott Fitzgerald's *Tales of the Jazz Age* is published.
- German Shepherd Rin Tin Tin appears in his first movie, *The Man From Hell's River*.
- Insulin is introduced as a treatment for diabetes.
- Isadora Duncan introduces her style of free-form dance at Carnegie Hall.
- King Tut's tomb is discovered in Egypt.
- The Lincoln Memorial is dedicated in Washington, DC.
- Mussolini becomes dictator of Italy.
- The National Football League is created (from the American Pro Football Association).
- Radio begins daily broadcasts of music, news, and Sunday sermons in New York.
- *Readers Digest* begins publication.
- Sigmund Freud publishes *Beyond the Pleasure Principle*.
- Snow falls in Tucson, Arizona! A one-day *and* one-month record of six inches in March.
- Speakeasies number an estimated five thousand in New York.
- The U.S. Supreme Court unanimously upholds women's right to vote.
- Technicolor System 2 debuts with the movie *Toll of the Sea*.
- Tex Guinan takes a job as speakeasy hostess in NYC; her catchphrase: "Hello, sucker!"
- James Joyce's *Ulysses* is published.
- The U.S.S.R. is formed out of fourteen republics under the dictatorship of Vladimir Lenin.
- Walt Disney begins his first film company: Laugh-O-Gram.
- Warren Harding becomes the first U.S. President to broadcast a speech on the radio.

Sopa de Tomate
Tomato Soup
"Served since 1922"

Monica served tomato soup every Friday from the time she opened El Charro in 1922. With a tostada grande, it makes a great Mexican version of the classic American soup 'n' sandwich lunch. On hot summer days, this soup can be transformed into gazpacho by adding chopped tomatoes, cucumbers, and peppers, and Worcestershire sauce or Tabasco sauce to taste. Carlotta also suggests that it can be frozen in ice cube trays, then used in lieu of water-based ice for Bloody Mary cocktails.

1	quart water		1	tablespoon garlic purée (page 93)
2	cups beef stock (or 2 additional cups water)		¾	cup sugar
2	tablespoons oil		12	ounces evaporated milk (or nonfat evaporated milk)
2	tablespoons flour			
3	cups canned tomato purée (or substitute 1½ cups water mixed with 1½ cups canned tomato paste)		**GARNISH:**	
			4	hard-cooked eggs, chopped (optional)
½	cup minced white onion		1	cup chopped parsley
1	teaspoon salt		1	cup crumbled totopos (corn chips, page 113)

In an 8-quart stockpot, bring water and stock to the boil. Meanwhile, in a skillet, lightly brown the flour in oil over low heat. Stir the browned flour into the boiling stock. After cooking the mixture 10 minutes until slightly thickened, add the tomato purée, onion, salt, garlic, and sugar. Add the evaporated milk. Set the soup aside 10 minutes to allow the flavors to blend. Taste and adjust the seasonings. Garnish with chopped eggs, parsley, and totopos.

[Low-fat notita: To lower the fat and calories, substitute nonfat evaporated milk, or even water, and eliminate or diminish the amount of chopped-egg garnish.]

MAKES 6 TO 8 SERVINGS

Sopa de Camote y Calabasa
Sweet Potato and Pumpkin Soup

In the spirit of harvest time, this earthy soup is especially satisfying when made with freshly roasted green chiles from the autumn crop. It is hearty and sweet, and if made with vegetable stock, purely vegetarian.

3	pounds of sweet potatoes
½	cup margarine or butter
1	medium onion, chopped
6	cups vegetable or chicken broth
1	large can of pumpkin purée
2	cups of canned milk
½	cup brown sugar
1	tablespoon garlic purée (page 93)
1	cup of chopped green chiles (optional)
2	cups of frozen kernel corn (white or yellow)
½	tablespoon cinnamon
½	tablespoon nutmeg

Cook the sweet potatoes in the oven or boil in water until they are done. Once cooked, peel and reserve. Melt the margarine in a large pot. Sautée the onion, then add the broth of your choice. Add the potatoes, pumpkin purée, milk, sugar, and garlic. Bring to a simmer. After heating for 15 minutes, remove and cool. Place the cooled soup in a blender and blend to desired consistency, adding water or milk if needed to thin it. Finish by adding green chiles, and corn kernels. In a separate bowl combine the cinnamon and nutmeg and sprinkle on top. (Carlotta recommends garnishing with cinnamon bread croutons.)

MAKES 4 TO 6 SERVINGS

Sopa de Marisco
Shellfish Soup

This hearty seafood soup requires nothing but a garnish of El Charro salsa picante and perhaps a warm flour tortilla for dipping to be a full and satisfying meal. Scallops may be used in place of, or in addition to the shrimp.

2	tablespoons cooking oil	1	cup diced green chile
1	cup finely chopped white onion	1	cup diced fresh tomatoes
1	tablespoon garlic purée (page 93)	½	cup fresh chopped cilantro
8	cups of water	1	pound skinned white cod fish (cut into 1 inch cubes)
1	tablespoon salt	1	pound fresh raw medium shrimp shelled and deveined
1	tablespoon pepper		
2	cups of canned, stewed tomatoes	**GARNISH:**	
½	cup of diced red chile peppers		Lime wedges
1	cup diced celery		Fresh cut cilantro
1	cup frozen peas		Green onions
1	cup diced carrots		Red chile flakes

In a large stockpot heat the oil over medium heat, and then add the chopped white onion and garlic. Saute until the onion turns tender and golden brown. Add 8 cups of water and the salt, pepper, canned tomatoes, chile peppers, celery, peas, carrots, green chile, fresh tomatoes, and cilantro. Simmer until all the flavors have melded together (about 10 minutes). Raise the heat to high and begin to add seafood. Heat the soup to a rolling boil, then lower the temperature to medium and allow the fish to cook another 5 minutes. Remove the fish from the heat, and once the soup has cooled a bit, season the recipe to taste and garnish with lime wedges, fresh cut cilantro, green onions and red chile flakes.

MAKES 8 TO 10 SERVINGS

Caldo de Queso
Cheese and Potato Soup

Rough-cut potatoes and stringy cheese make this a soul-satisfier. Puréed and topped with a spoonful of tomato salsa, it's elegant. *Caldo de Queso* may be refrigerated for use the next day, or frozen for later use.

4	medium potatoes, peeled and cubed
5	cups water
3	cups beef stock
1	medium white onion, sliced and separated
1	teaspoon salt
½	cup garlic purée (page 93)
8	fresh Anaheim chiles, roasted (page 79) chopped
1¼	cups milk or evaporated milk
2	large tomatoes, coarsely chopped
4	cups cubed or shredded longhorn cheese or crumbled Mexican cheese

---

In an 8-quart stockpot, cook the potatoes in the water until soft. Remove the potatoes with a slotted spoon and set aside. Add the beef stock to the potato water, and bring to a boil. Add the onion, salt, garlic purée, chiles, and milk. Simmer 10 minutes. Taste and adjust the seasoning, adding more chiles, if you like. Add the cooked potatoes and tomatoes and simmer for about 10 minutes. To serve, place ½ cup cubed cheese in each warmed bowl and ladle the soup over the cheese.

[Low-fat notita: Low-fat or fat-free cheese and nonfat condensed milk make an acceptable, lighter soup.]

MAKES 6 TO 8 SERVINGS

Posole

Pork and Hominy Soup

A dish with soul and character from Jalisco, home of mariachi music. Carlotta says that in Jalisco, a traditional posole will contain oxtails and pigs' heads. "Our family has settled for cubed boneless pork," she points out. She also notes that it is possible to make vegetarian posole simply by eliminating the pork.

Hominy is a common grocery item in the Southwest, where it is found in bags at the meat counter. It is white corn kernels processed in slaked lime so they puff up to three times their normal size. Outside the Southwest, you can buy hominy in cans (but canned hominy cannot be used to make corn tortilla masa).

1	pound whole hominy, rinsed well	4	cups cooked pinto beans (page 66)
5	cups cold water	2	cups strained beef broth, or reserved pork broth
2	pounds boneless pork, cut into 4 pieces	2	whole dried red chiles, seeded, chopped
3	cups cold water	2	whole fresh Anaheim chiles, chopped
2	whole heads garlic, partially separated		
2	tablespoons oil	**GARNISH:**	
2	medium onions, chopped		Chopped tomatoes
1	tablespoon crushed oregano		Oregano
1	tablespoon salt, or to taste		Salsa

In a covered stockpot, simmer the hominy in the 5 cups water for 4 hours, until kernels burst open ("flower") and are tender. Add hot water as necessary. In another pot, simmer the pork in the 3 cups water with the garlic about 30 minutes, or until tender. Cool and drain, reserving the broth. Cut the meat into ¾-inch cubes and set aside.

While the meat is cooling, heat the vegetable oil in a large skillet. Lightly brown the onions in the oil. Add the cubed pork and oregano to the hominy mixture and simmer 2 more hours. Taste and season with salt. Add the cooked pinto beans to the broth, stir, and adjust seasoning. Add the chiles and stir gently. Serve in large soup bowls; garnish with chopped tomatoes, oregano, and salsa.

MAKES 8 TO 12 SERVINGS

Sopa de Ajo
Garlic Soup

What a wonderful gift of nature garlic is! We have recently added a number of books to our gift shop, and Charlotte has brought in several wonderful garlic cookbooks. Looking at them inspired me and reminded me of this recipe for garlic soup that Monica made, simply called *Sopa de Ajo* (Garlic Soup). Originally, it was used for medicinal purposes; however, I think it might make a comeback—at least with me. It definitely has a bite to it, and one of my employees suggested that it might be good in a flask.

2	tablespoons butter	1	tablespoon salt
1	tablespoon olive oil	1	tablespoon pepper
6	large white onions, thinly sliced	⅓	cup brandy
10	plus 6 cloves of garlic	6	bollios (French rolls), thickly sliced
1	teaspoon Mexican oregano		
⅓	cup flour	4	cups grated casero or panela cheese (or a combination of Monterey Jack and mozzarella)
1	cup white wine		
2	quarts strained chicken broth (vegetable broth can also be substituted)		

Melt the butter with the olive oil in a large soup pot. Add the onions, and cook until soft. Finely chop the 10 cloves garlic and add to the onions with the oregano; cook, while stirring frequently, for about 25 minutes. Sprinkle the flour over the onions and stir until blended. Pour in the wine and the strained broth; bring to a boil. Add the salt and pepper. Skim the top and let simmer for flavor, blending for about 30 minutes. Stir in the brandy. In a skillet lightly brown the remaining 6 garlic cloves in some margarine. Arrange six ovenproof soup bowls on a cookie sheet. Ladle the soup, filling the bowls half full. Add a browned garlic clove to each bowl of soup. Toast, butter, and garlic the bollios. Place a bollio in each bowl. Top the bread with the grated cheese and broil for about 2 minutes, or until the cheese is melted. Serve immediately.

You can leave out this last step, pack the bread up, and drink the hot garlic and onion toddy soup right from your flask. You can also add cooked chicken, white fish, shrimp, or vegetables to create a delicious soup.

MAKES 10 TO 12 SERVINGS

Sopa de Tortilla
Tortilla Soup

Tortilla soup can be a light appetizer or a filling meal. For the former, make the recipe as follows. For a supperweight soup, add a cup of cooked, shredded chicken meat before serving. El Charro serves tortilla soup in a thick, earthenware pot; it comes garnished with crisp tortilla chips, slivers of fresh-cut avocado, and a light sprinkle of white Mexican cheese.

6	cups chicken broth (skimmed)
1	tablespoon oil
1	cup chopped white onion
2	bell peppers, chopped
2	cups chopped tomatoes
2	cups chopped green chiles
1	tablespoon garlic purée (page 93)
1	tablespoon oregano
1	tablespoon pepper
2	tablespoons seasoning salt, optional

GARNISH:

6	small corn tortillas, cut lengthwise and fried until crisp
2	cups shredded white cheese, such as Monterey Jack
2	avocados, pitted, peeled, and diced
½	cup chopped green onions, green part only
3	tablespoons chopped cilantro, optional

In a large pot bring the broth to a boil; reduce the heat to simmer. In a saucepan heat the oil, and sauté the onion, bell peppers, tomatoes, green chiles, and garlic purée until lightly translucent. Add to the simmering broth. Add the oregano, pepper, and seasoning salt, if using. Cover the pot and simmer for 20 minutes.

To serve: In each bowl place ⅓ cup cheese. Add the broth and one-sixth of the diced avocado. Garnish with the green onions, the cilantro, if using, and float tortilla strips on top.

MAKES 6 SERVINGS

Tucson Timeline

The history of life in the Tucson Valley begins ca. 10,000 B.C. with the migrations of Paleoindian and Archaic hunters and gatherers. Whether or not there was continuous habitation is unclear, though evidence of agricultural settlements along the Santa Cruz River have been found dating from ca. 1000 B.C.

Between A.D. 200 and 1450, the Hohokam culture thrives. The Pima and Tohono O'odham are the descendents of that advanced civilization and have inhabited the region since the Hohokam decline.

Around 1540 the Coronado Expedition crosses Arizona in search of the "Seven Cities of Gold."

Father Francisco Kino establishes the Mission San Xavier del Bac in 1699. It won't be until 1797 that it will be completed.

The Mission San Agustin, a "visita" of San Xavier, is established on the west bank of the Santa Cruz River in 1757. The construction of the mission and the convento is completed in the 1790s.

In 1775 Hugo O'Conor—a red-haired Irishman who had joined the Spanish army and was known as The Red Captain—establishes the Tucson Presido at the site of the mission once called St. Augustin. This year marks the official birthdate of the City of Tucson.

Tucson becomes part of Mexico when it fights for independence in 1821. After the Gadsden Purchase in 1854, Tucson falls under the jurisdiction of the United States.

Arizona becomes an official territory in 1863. Between 1867 and 1889, Tucson holds the title of territorial capitol.

Tucson's first Catholic Cathedral, San Augustin.

In 1880 the Southern Pacific Railroad reaches Tucson. The population reaches 8,000.

In 1882 Bishop Jean Baptiste Salpointe asks French stonemason Jules Flin to come to Tucson to carve the portal for the city's first Catholic cathedral, San Agustín. Flin's work, including St. Mary's Hospital and St. Joseph's Academy earned him the title *El Leon de Piedra* (The Lion of Stone).

In 1884 Flin married Carlota Brunet; and their eight children included Monica Flin, founder of El Charro.

Arizona becomes the 48th state in the Union in 1912.

Monica Flin opens El Charro Café in 1922.

By 1950 Tucson's population has reached 120,000 and by 1960 it nearly doubled to 220,000. The City and Pima County officially recognize the city's history by adopting historic district ordinances in 1972.

Tucson becomes the 30th largest U.S. city in 2000 as its population tops 480,000.

From *Yesterday's Tucson Today.*
Copyright © 1996 by Harry Cuming.
Used by permission.

Monica Flin in 1950 with her six waitresses.

Sopa de Campanas Mixtas
Mixed-Pepper Bisque

Campana means "bell" in Spanish; and the campanas here are different-colored bell peppers along with spicier roasted Anaheims. Fresh-roasted Anaheims are best, imparting a true-West earthy character to the pepper puree. This is a soup that is good both hot (in cool weather) and cold (as a refresher in the Tucson summer).

PEPPER PURÉE:

6   bell peppers, red, green, and gold

2   fresh Anaheim chiles, roasted (page 79)

1   onion, chopped

2   carrots, chopped

BISQUE:

3   cups broth

1   cup water

1   cup milk or cream

1   cup chopped green onion

¼   cup garlic purée (page 93)

2   cups cubed, cooked potatoes

1   cup cubed, cooked squash

½   cup chopped fresh basil

¼   teaspoon freshly ground black pepper

First, cut wafer-thin slices from each pepper to garnish the bisque. Set aside. Remove and discard the seeds and veins from the remaining peppers, and chop. Place the chopped peppers along with the chiles, onion, and carrots in a large kettle of boiling water, and simmer until soft. Drain. Purée the vegetables in a blender or food processor.

To make the bisque, bring the broth, water, milk, onion, garlic purée, potatoes, squash, basil, and black pepper to a boil. Reduce the heat. Slowly add the pepper purée, stirring constantly, and allow to simmer (not boil) for 10 minutes to reduce slightly and blend the flavors. Serve in warm bowls, and garnish with the reserved pepper slivers.

MAKES 6 TO 8 SERVINGS

Sopa de Purée de Papas
Mashed Potato Soup

The smoky flavor of chipotle chiles makes this rich-as-cream comfort-food soup into something exciting and wonderful. Carlotta proposes making a low-fat version by using non-fat milk and sour cream.

1	onion, chopped
	Vegetable oil spray
2	cups chicken stock or water
1½	cups milk
3	pounds new or red potatoes, cubed
1	tablespoon margarine
1	(15-ounce) can creamed corn
¼	cup garlic purée
	Salt and pepper
	2 chipotle chiles

GARNISH:

Tortilla chips

Sour cream

Green onions, chopped

Coat a stockpot with vegetable oil spray, and sauté the onion quickly. Add a little water, and sweat the onion. Add the chicken stock or water, milk, margarine, and cubed potatoes. Cook uncovered until potatoes are tender. Drain, and transfer to a food processor or blender. Add the creamed corn and garlic purée and blend until smooth. (This can be done in batches if your processor is small.) Return to the pot. Cut the chipotles into ¼-inch pieces, and then grind them with a mortar and pestle—or by working a fork against the bottom and sides of a rough-textured bowl—until they form a paste. Stir into the potato mixture and bring to a boil. Ladle the bisque into the bowls and garnish with baked tortilla chips and dollops of sour cream mixed with the chopped green onions.

MAKES 6 TO 8 SERVINGS

Sopa Seca de Fideo
Vermicelli Soup

This is a forgiving recipe that invites the cook to take it in whatever direction feels right at the time. Basically it is noodles and tomatoes, flavored to taste, with cheese of choice. "A catch-all recipe," Carlotta calls it, with variations "from macaroni and cheese to any number of casseroles."

¼	cup oil
2	pounds coiled fideos (vermicelli)
1	cup tomato sauce
1	teaspoon salt, or to taste
¼	cup garlic purée (page 93)
1	white onion, chopped
6	cups hot chicken or beef stock
½	cup chopped bell pepper
1	cup chopped fresh tomato
1	cup shredded longhorn cheese, or other cheese

GARNISH:

1	cup shredded additional cheese

Heat the oil in a skillet, and lightly brown the fideos coils on both sides. Transfer to a 4-quart saucepan. Add the tomato sauce, salt, garlic purée, onion, stock, bell pepper, and tomato and simmer over low heat 20 minutes. Stir once or twice, separating the coils with a long fork. Continue cooking, uncovered, until all the liquid has been absorbed. Add the cheese and stir. Garnish with additional cheese.

MAKES 6 TO 8 SERVINGS

Rice, Pasta, Beans & Vegetables

(Arroz, Fideos, Frijoles y Verduras)

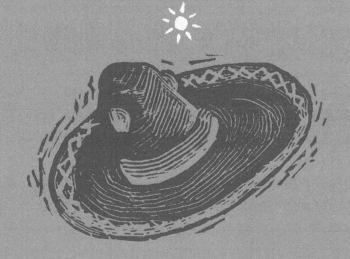

Carlotta attributes the ubiquity of rice in the Mexican diet to the influence of early Asian immigrants; and yet she is mystified by the use of the term "Spanish rice" to describe rice steamed with a confetti of vegetables. Rice is a staple on Mexican-style plates virtually everywhere in North America, as are beans; but one of the more distinctive and truly Mexican ways of serving starch is in a *sopa seca*. This is a self-contradictory-sounding term that means "dry soup"; and it usually refers to a dish based on rice or pasta that is cooked with stock and other ingredients until the liquid is merely moisture in a dish that is more like a stew than a soup. Spanish *paella* is one example of a *sopa seca;* but at El Charro, it is pasta that stars in the favorite variation, *Sopa Seca de Fideo* (p. 52). Carlotta attributes its popularity to the fact that Mexico City is home to some of the world's best Italian restaurants.

Arroz Estilo El Charro
El Charro Rice with Tomato

El Charro Rice is not like ordinary rice. It is tender and slightly starchy, but what makes it special is the way it absorbs the flavors of the vegetables with which it is cooked. While it is generally served as a side dish, Carlotta informs us that the addition of cooked chicken or shrimp transforms it into a hearty main course.

2	tablespoons oil
1	small onion, chopped
2	cups uncooked rice
1	teaspoon salt, or to taste
4	cups stock, or half stock, half water
1	tablespoon ground hot red chile (optional)
½	cup tomato sauce
½	cup garlic purée (page 93)
1	cup frozen peas and carrots
1	tomato, chopped

Heat the oil in a large skillet. Lightly brown the onion. Add the rice and stir constantly over low heat until the rice starts to brown. (Be careful not to let it get too brown.) Add the salt and stock. Add the ground red chile, if using. Increase the heat, and bring to a boil; reduce the heat, cover tightly and simmer 10 minutes. Add the tomato sauce, garlic purée, peas, carrots, and chopped tomato and stir. Cover and cook about 20 minutes, or until the rice is tender. Uncover during the last few minutes of cooking if you want the rice to be on the dry side. Let rice sit for 15 minutes, and then fluff it with two forks.

[Variation: Add cooked chicken or shrimp, or both, for a hearty main dish.]

[Notita: A piece of foil under the cover will help create a tight fit so the rice steams to perfection.]

MAKES 6 TO 8 SERVINGS

Arroz con Plátanos
White Rice with Bananas

In the El Charro kitchen, the earthy and spicy nature of the cuisine is shot through with a vein of sweetness. Carlotta believes that this particular recipe for white rice with bananas probably originated with the Chinese cook her father's family employed; but it has since become a Flores family favorite. "I recently used it as a stuffing for a chimichanga and it was a big hit," she says. She also likes to remind the cook that the fruity flavor of the bananas is well-balanced by a shot of hot mustard added to the recipe.

⅓	*cup oil*
2	*firm green bananas (or plantains)*
3	*cups cooked rice*

Heat the oil in a deep skillet. Peel and slice the bananas or plantains diagonally into ½-inch pieces. Fry in the hot oil, turning once, until light brown. Serve atop bowls of hot rice.

MAKES 8 SERVINGS

Arroz con Fruta
Rice Flavored with Fruit

The sweetness of the fruit in the rice is especially appealing when served with a *picante*-sauced meat, such as Pork Tenderloin with Mango.

2	*cups rice*
4	*cups water*
½	*teaspoon salt*

FRUIT:

Dried cranberries or raisins

Chopped prunes, apricots, or pineapple

Orange or tangerine segments

Wash the rice in cold water. Drain. Place in a heavy 2-quart saucepan. Add the 4 cups water. Cover and bring to the boil. Quickly stir in ¼ to 1 cup fruit of your choice. Cover immediately and reduce the heat to the lowest setting; cook until the rice is tender and water is absorbed. Let sit covered off heat for several minutes. Fluff with a fork before serving.

[Notita: Leftover rice becomes a healthful snack when topped with plain yogurt.]

MAKES 6 SERVINGS

Berenjena y Cilantro Crema
Eggplant with Cilantro Cream

Cilantro is a controversial herb – you love its musky flavor or you hate it – and exactly what it is can be a little confusing. The leaf that Mexican cooks know as *cilantro* comes from the same plant known in other recipes as Chinese parsley, the seed of which is coriander. They all have that same assertive flavor that works well (if you like it) singing harmony with spicy dishes and as a counterpoint to those that are creamy and mild . . . like this eggplant with cilantro cream.

¼	cup margarine
1	large eggplant, peeled, sliced, sweated, and diced
1	teaspoon salt
1	quart sour cream
1	cup chopped cilantro
½	cup chopped parsley
¼	cup garlic purée (page 93)
¼	cup purple onion
1	tablespoon plus 1 teaspoon paprika
½	cup sliced pimiento-stuffed green olives
	Juice of 1 lemon
	Fresh oregano leaves (not dried)
	Flour tortillas
	Butter
	Sesame seeds

In a sauté pan melt the margarine. Add the eggplant and salt and cook al dente. Cool and reserve to add to other ingredients. Place the sour cream in a bowl. Add the cilantro, parsley, garlic, onion, 1 tablespoon paprika, olives, lemon juice, and oregano leaves; mix together. Add the eggplant, and blend together. Refrigerate and serve in a hollowed out eggplant. Garnish with the remaining teaspoon of paprika and serve with soft flour tortilla wedges that have been brushed with butter and sesame seeds and then toasted.

MAKES 6 TO 8 SERVINGS

Mexican Independence Day

In the United States *Cinco de Mayo* (pages 96–97) is often mistakenly thought of as the anniversary of Mexico's independence, but for Mexicans—and Tucsonans who feel close to Mexico—May 5 is only a secondary holiday. The real day to celebrate is September 16. That date is known as Mexican Independence Day, and it has all the emotional potency of July 4 in the U.S. At El Charro, it is an extra-special occasion because September 16, 1972, was the day that the Flores family reopened the historic restaurant.

On September 16, 1810, Father Miguel Hidalgo y Costilla, the original leader of the Mexican people against the rule of Spain, rang the bell of the little church in the village of Dolores and proclaimed his country's rebellion. (Mexico was later conquered by France, the defeat of which in 1862 is commemorated on *Cinco de Mayo*.) The War of Independence lasted ten years.

Now, late in the evening every September 15 and into September 16, it is traditional to remember Hidalgo's "*Grito de Dolores*," a cry for freedom in which he is supposed to have said, "Long live our Lady of Guadalupe! Long live independence!" *El Grito*, as it is called, is cause for all manner of festivity, including fireworks, dancing in the streets, and patriotic toasts. Men wear traditional charro outfits and outrageous sombreros, and women don wild, colorful dresses. Mariachi bands play, and everyone eats, drinks, and makes merry.

"You have to have a party on Mexican Independence Day," Raymon Flores declares. "We serve three-colored cookies to symbolize the flag of Mexico; we have red, white, and green enchiladas, and even layered margaritas like the flag." The traditional toast, when hoisting one of those margaritas, is *¡Viva Mexico!*

Calabacitas con Queso
Squash with Cheese

Other than the fact that the cheese should be added just before serving, this recipe has no ironclad rules. Adjust and alter it to your taste. Almost any kind of small squash can be used—zucchini, pan-patty, yellow crookneck—singly or in combination; and if you like it really zesty, feel free to use a chile hotter than Anaheim. Use small strips of colorful roasted peppers to garnish each serving.

Carlotta notes that leftover *Calabacitas* can be puréed and blended with beef stock, milk, and seasonings to taste to make *Sopa de Calabacitas*. For a vegetarian version of the *sopa*, substitute 1 percent milk or canned low-fat milk for the beef stock.

2	tablespoons oil
1	white onion, chopped
10	medium squash, cut into 1-inch chunks
3	tomatoes, chopped
¼	cup garlic purée (page 93)
¼	cup water
2	fresh Anaheim chiles, roasted (page 79) chopped
1	(8-ounce) can kernel corn, drained
½	pound longhorn cheese, shredded
	Salt and pepper

In a large skillet heat the oil and sauté the onion, squash, tomatoes, and garlic purée. Add the water, cover, and cook over low heat 20 minutes. When the squash is tender, add the chopped chiles and corn, and stir slightly. Season with salt and pepper to taste. Cook 5 minutes more. Turn off the heat. Immediately sprinkle with the cheese; then cover for a few minutes so the cheese melts.

[Notita: Calabacitas can be prepared and refrigerated ahead of serving, up to the point of adding the cheese. When ready to serve, warm the squash mixture slowly over low heat; then stir in the cheese, cover, and set aside 5 minutes.]

MAKES 6 TO 8 SERVINGS

Calabaza Dulce
Sweet Banana Squash

A multi-purpose dish that can be served warm or cool, as a side to spicy meat or as dessert after an earthy meal. If serving *Calabaza Dulce* for dessert, garnish it with whipped cream and chopped nuts.

3	pounds banana squash
1	cup brown sugar, or 1 cone piloncillo
¾	cup water

GARNISH:

1	cup heavy cream, whipped (sweetened if desired)
1¼	cups chopped nuts

Clean and peel the squash and remove the seeds. Cut into 2-inch cubes. In a 4-quart saucepan bring the squash, brown sugar, and water to a boil. Lower the heat; cover and simmer for 15 to 20 minutes. Uncover and cook for 15 minutes more, or until the squash is tender. Mash; adjust the seasonings. Serve warm or chilled topped with the whipped cream and nuts.

MAKES 6 TO 8 SERVINGS

Chiles Rellenos
Stuffed Chiles

Chiles rellenos depends on chiles. Use big, gentle Anaheims and it is a creamy meal; use pasillas or anchos and it's a dish with bite. That is the point of *Chiles Rellenos*: to celebrate the chile pepper, whatever its variety. That is why this dish is made with *fresh* chiles. Carlotta says that while cheese is always the proper garnish, the chiles may be stuffed not only with cheese, but also with ground chicken, *chorizo*, or tuna.

8	fresh Anaheim chiles, roasted (page 79), stems intact, if possible
1	pound Mexican or longhorn cheese, cut in strips

BATTER:

3	eggs
3	tablespoons flour
1	teaspoon salt
1	teaspoon ground black pepper
¼	cup oil

GARNISH:

4	cups Taco Sauce (page 88) warmed
2	cups shredded longhorn cheese

Make a 2-inch slit in the chiles and insert a strip of cheese. Set aside. Separate the eggs and beat the whites until stiff. Separately beat the yolks and fold them into the whites, along with the flour, salt, and pepper. Meanwhile, heat the oil in a large skillet. Dip the stuffed chiles, one at a time, into the egg batter to coat; then remove the chiles with a large spoon. Carefully lower the coated chiles into the hot oil, 3 or 4 at a time. Fry until golden brown on both sides.

To serve, arrange on a platter or individual plates, and pour the warm *Taco Sauce* over each chile. Garnish with more cheese, and place under the broiler to melt the cheese, if desired.

[Notita: The chiles may be made ahead to this point and reheated in a 400°F (205°C) oven about 10 minutes before adding topping.]

[Notita: Chicken, chorizo, or tuna may be used to stuff the chiles, but cheese is always a garnish.]

MAKES 4 TO 8 SERVINGS

Ejotes con Chile Colorado
String Beans with Red Chile Sauce

We enjoy this spicy green-bean dish with a plate of warm flour tortillas, or wrapped in tortillas, burro-style," Carlotta says. Another vegetarian triumph of the El Charro kitchen, red chili with string beans is good not only as burro filling, but also as a side dish for carne seca or other meat. Or it is possible to mix a couple of cups of cooked, cubed chicken into the cooked beans and top each hot serving with a good amount of shredded cheese, creating a knife-and-fork main course.

½   cup vegetable oil
¼   cup garlic purée (page 93)
2   cups Enchilada Sauce (page 90)
    Salt and pepper
1   pound fresh or frozen green beans, cut and cooked

Heat the oil, garlic purée, and *Salsa de Chile Colorado* in a large skillet. Cook over very low heat for 15 minutes, stirring frequently to prevent scorching. Add the cooked beans and heat through.

MAKES 6 TO 8 SERVINGS

Calendars

Other than its food, probably the best-known thing about El Charro is its calendar. Every year since Monica's time, the restaurant has given out a calendar with its name and a spectacular work of art above the months. Now, many years' worth of these calendars are displayed on the restaurant's walls.

The calendar art is flamboyantly Mexican: tableaux of bare-chested, muscle-bound Aztec men and swooningly beautiful women whose peasant blouses are always on the verge of revealing a bit too much. Nearly all the women resemble Ava Gardner: luscious red lips, elegant hands, golden earrings, and bright flowers in their ink-black long hair. They are buxom yet lithe, seductive yet innocent. The comely men and women are depicted in stormy landscapes of Wagnerian drama that are heroic, patriotic, and erotic all at once. Some of the best ones feature the work of artist Jesus Helguera and are printed in Mexico on shiny stock. The art is chosen each year by Ray Flores Sr.

The images on the calendars fall into a few general categories: beautiful mortals and Aztec gods and goddesses; spiritual depictions of Jesus, Saint Augustine, and the especially popular Virgin of Guadalupe; Saint of the Americas; couples courting; the happy home; pop-culture icons such as bullfighter Manolete; and patriotic odes to Mexico. One good example of an El Charro calendar is titled *"Iztaccihutal"* ("Sleeping Woman"). The picture is from a legend that goes back to pre-Columbian Mexico. It tells about a beautiful woman named Mixtli and her suitor, a poor but noble man who goes off to fight for her hand and returns to find his beloved dead because she could not live without him. Hoping the snow will awaken her, he takes her lifeless body to a volcanic

mountain top. Eventually, though, snow covers both lovers. That volcano outside Mexico City remains a testament to their undying love.

The popularity of El Charro's calendars was once the subject of an *Arizona Daily Star* article that described just how devoted the restaurant's calendar lovers can be. "One University student who was a fanatic about getting Aztec calendars would stare at them for hours," the story read. "And one man was so eager to have a calendar on the wall that he actually climbed on top of a table where people were eating."

It was Ray Flores's idea to post the giveaway calendars on the restaurant walls. He says it was just a way to occupy otherwise uninteresting wall space. But their strength as décor gave them a whole new meaning—and a desirability among customers that makes the distribution of each year's calendar an eagerly awaited event. What once was mere wall covering has wound up a whole new way to appreciate El Charro Café. And now, when grateful customers bring gifts to Carlotta, chances are good they will bring images of saints that reflect the spirit of the calendars.

Frijoles de la Olla
Whole Beans

The staple beans of El Charro are served with nearly every meal that comes from the kitchen. Much can be done to fancy them up, but as a companion to interesting, complex, and colorfully-flavored dishes, simple is what's required. Carlotta also warns, "Stirring beans clouds the broth." A few other basic suggestions:

- Adding cold water to cooking beans will darken them. Add only boiling water.
- If you add salt to beans too early as they cook, they will toughen. Add salt only after the beans are at least half-cooked. And don't forget that as the liquid boils away, the saltiness will intensify. Adjust the taste when ready to serve.
- It is not necessary to presoak beans before cooking.
- Refrigerating hot beans makes them sour. Spread them on a roasting pan soaking in water to insure sweetness.

2	cups pinto beans	**Fresh-Tomato Condiment**	
2	quarts cold water	2	fresh tomatoes, chopped
1	whole head garlic, peeled and mashed	1	tablespoon fresh oregano
	Salt		Sprinkle of white vinegar
			Dab of sour cream (optional)
		1	onion, chopped

Pick over the beans carefully, discarding any debris, and rinse the beans thoroughly. Place in an 8-quart stockpot with the water. Add the garlic and bring to a boil. Immediately reduce heat, and cook slowly, undisturbed, until the beans are very tender, at least 2 hours. Salt lightly to taste and serve with the fresh tomato condiment.

To make the fresh tomato condiment, mix together the tomatoes, oregano, vinegar, sour cream, and onion.

[Variation: You will often find beans cooked with ham hocks or bacon, onion, and spiced with oregano or, in Texas, cumin. Sometimes it's hard to leave them simple.]

MAKES 6 TO 8 SERVINGS

El Charro Frijoles Refritos
Refried Beans

Yes, it is possible to make refried beans with canola oil instead of lard; but to traditionalists, the true joy of this classic side dish is the rich flavor that lard imparts—the more lard, the more delicious the *frijoles*. Ray Flores Sr. recalls, "My mother made the best refried beans, which she called *frijoles chinitos*. They were beans like we wouldn't dare make today because of all the extra lard. She had them in the skillet and she kept cooking and mashing and adding lard. They got darker and darker and she spun them with a spoon because you couldn't let them sit for even a minute in the pan; and when you were done, you had the most delicious refried beans in the world."

4	cups cooked pinto beans (page 66)
2	tablespoons melted lard, hot bacon fat, or canola oil
1	(12-ounce) can evaporated milk
½	pound longhorn cheese or Mexican cheese, shredded
	Enchilada Sauce (page 90)
	Additional lard, bacon fat, or oil

Mash the cooked beans in a skillet and add the hot lard or bacon fat. Mix well. Stir in the evaporated milk. Cook over very low heat, stirring frequently.

[Variation: Beans can be served at this point, without the cheese, salsa, or additional fat. Or the cheese, salsa, and lard can be added and the beans truly "refried" in a bit more smoking-hot fat just before serving.]

MAKES 6 TO 8 SERVINGS

Hongos
Mushrooms

This can be a great side dish or a wonderful burrito stuffing for your vegetarian family and friends.

⅓	*cup margarine or oil*
1	*pound medium whole mushrooms, rinsed and cleaned*
1	*red bell pepper*
1	*green bell pepper*
1	*medium yellow onion, chopped*
1	*tablespoon chopped garlic or garlic purée (page 93)*
	cojita cheese (optional)

Melt the margarine in a pan. Add the mushrooms, peppers, onion, and garlic. Lightly sauté the mixture, but do not overcook. Peppers should be crisp. Sprinkle with the *cojita* cheese.

MAKES 4 SERVINGS

Quelites con Frijoles
Spinach and Beans

Quelite, also known as *espinaca*, is spinach—a favorite side dish all year around at El Charro, but especially as part of the vegetable-focused Lenten dinners. This simple recipe for spinach and beans is a vegetarian's delight. It can be served as is, with rice on the side, or as the filling for enchiladas or chalupas. If you sprinkle it with crumbled cheese and add a spoonful of salsa picante, then wrap that in a tortilla, you have a spinach burro.

4	*bunches fresh spinach, or 2 (10-ounce) packages frozen chopped spinach*
1	*tablespoon oil*
½	*cup minced white onion*
1	*tablespoon garlic purée (page 93)*
½	*cup crumbled Mexican cheese*
½	*cup half-and-half*
1	*cup Frijoles de la Olla (whole cooked pinto beans, page 66)*

Rinse the fresh spinach, and steam 10 minutes in a small amount of water. Drain and chop. Thaw, cook, and drain, if using frozen spinach. In a large skillet, sauté the onions in the oil until translucent. Add the garlic purée. Stir in the spinach and cheese. Stir in the half-and-half, and boil 3 minutes. Add the beans and simmer a few minutes.

[Variation: Substitute spinach and nuts for enchiladas. Eliminate the pinto beans in Quelites con Frijoles *and add about ½ cup chopped walnuts or pecans. Place the filling on softened corn tortillas, roll, and place seam side down in a baking dish. Top with Enchilada Sauce (page 90) and cheese. Bake at 325°F (165°C) until the cheese bubbles. Serve with rice flavored with chicken or vegetable stock and refried beans.]*

[Notita: Add a little crumbled cheese and a bit of salsa to the Quelites con Frijoles, *wrap it all in a tortilla, and you have a lovely spinach burro. Sometimes we use* quelites *blended with nuts and cheese as a filling for enchiladas.]*

MAKES 6 TO 8 SERVINGS

EL CHARRO CAFÉ COOKBOOK

Papas y Chiles
Fried Potatoes and Chiles for Taco Filling

El Charro is especially popular among vegetarians because so many of its best dishes are naturally meatless. The combination of fried potatoes and chiles makes a satisfying filling for tacos at any meal, including breakfast.

1	*pound new potatoes*
1	*tablespoon oil*
1	*onion, sliced*
2	*fresh Anaheim chiles, roasted (page 79)*
	Oil for sautéing
	Salt and pepper

Cut the potatoes and boil until cooked but firm. Peel, if desired. When cool enough to handle, slice coarsely and drain on paper toweling.In a large skillet, heat the oil. Sauté the sliced onion until soft, adding more oil if needed. Add the potatoes, shaking the pan to distribute the oil. Cook over medium heat, shaking the pan often until the potatoes are lightly browned. Stir in the diced chiles. Season with salt and pepper to taste. Use as a filling for tacos.

MAKES 4 TO 6 SERVINGS

Rajas con Crema y Piñones
Creamed Green Chiles with Pine Nuts

The *Rajas* in the name of this recipe means strips of green chile. The chiles are mild Anaheims, but their earthy savor combined with cream and sour cream gives this dish an intoxicating poise. Carlotta notes that the chile, onion, and garlic mixture can be prepared ahead and heated with cream, cheese, and pine nuts just before serving.

1	onion, sliced
¼	cup garlic purée (page 93)
12	fresh Anaheim chiles, roasted (page 79)
½	teaspoon salt (omit if using feta cheese)
1	cup cream, sour cream, or nonfat sour cream
½	cup crumbled Mexican or feta cheese
1	teaspoon dried oregano
1	tablespoon toasted piñones (optional)

Sauté the onion with the garlic in a nonstick skillet. Add the chile strips and salt, and sauté until warmed through. Add the cream and nonfat sour cream a little at a time, stirring carefully until the mixture is thick enough to cover the chiles. Add the oregano and crumbled cheese; stir.

To serve, sprinkle with piñones that have been toasted briefly in a dry skillet, if desired.

[Notita: Monica probably used homemade crème fraîche in these dishes. A facsimile of the rich French crème fraîche can be made by mixing heavy cream and nonfat sour cream. It is lighter in fat and calories and holds up well on steamed fresh spinach or carrots or other cooked vegetables. Mexican fresh cream is available in some southwestern supermarkets.]

MAKES 6 TO 8 SERVINGS

Chile Primer

Peppers" aren't really peppers at all. Like tomatoes, they don't quite fit any category of food. To botanists, they are berries; growers consider them fruit; chefs think of them as a vegetable. The word is spelled two other ways: *chile* is frequently used to refer to the plant rather than the dish, and *chili* usually refers to the dish rather than the plant.

While Tucson's Mexican fare is rarely four-alarm hot as in neighboring New Mexico, the flavor of chiles is fundamental. Here are thumbnail portraits of some of the most frequently encountered varieties:

Anaheim

The Anaheim is a large, thick-fleshed pepper with a mild, sunny flavor. It is available both green and red (ripened). The ripened anaheim is quite sweet, like a bell pepper with a more assertive personality.

Ancho

The ancho is a dried poblano chile with an earthy flavor and moderate heat. There is a zest to the ancho that makes it essential in *molé* and gives many chile dishes their buoyant charm.

Chipotle

A dried, smoked jalapeño, the chipotle is a siren song to serious chile-heads. Usually fairly hot, it is essential to many fiery southwestern bowls of red, and its distinctive smoky/sweet flavor becomes a dominant note in almost any dish in which it's used.

Habañero

About as hot as chile gets, the habañero is strictly for

chile-maniacs, and then only in itty-bitty pieces as a condiment. Unless you really like ferociously hot food, avoid it. But if you do like your chili hot, a little bit of finely minced habañero pepper—or hot sauce made from habañeros—will provide not only heat, but also the unusual tropical zest that no other pepper provides.

Jalapeño

The jalapeño is hot stuff, but not unbearable to most tongues. It is frequently served pickled and sliced, and generally used as a garnish for plates of nachos or green-chile cheeseburgers. The jalapeño has a powerful garden flavor, as well as heat.

New Mexico

Also known as the "long green," the New Mexico chile varies in heat level from mild to medium-hot. Large and thick-fleshed, it has a summer-sun flavor. Puréed New Mexican peppers are frequently served in bowls alongside other dishes as a dip for warm wheat tortillas, and they are often used as a marinade for meat that is to be grilled or baked.

Pasilla

A dark, dried pepper, the pasilla is medium-hot with a pickly taste that makes it a favorite to purée as the basis of more complicated chile recipes.

Poblano

So dark green it may appear black, the poblano chile ranges from moderately hot to three-alarm. It has thick-fleshed walls that make it wonderful for roasting, which brings out a profound, verdant flavor.

Relleno de Jalapeño
Savory Jalapeño Stuffing

This "stuffing" is in fact a multi-purpose recipe that can be a zesty vegetarian meal unto itself, an extra-spicy (non-vegetarian) casserole if you add a cup-and-a-half of cooked, crumbled *chorizo* (sausage), or stuffing for a turkey or pork loin. Carlotta also suggests using it to fill pockets cut into thick pork chops.

¼	pound (1 stick) margarine
1	cup chopped onion
½	cup chopped celery
3	loaves commercial, jalapeño-cheese bread, sliced
2	cups warm water
½	pound crumbled tomato-and-basil feta cheese

GARNISH (optional):

Strips of roasted red bell pepper

Jalapeño slices

Preheat the oven to 400°F (205°C). In a large skillet melt the margarine. Sauté the onion and celery, stirring frequently. Meanwhile lightly toast the slices of jalapeño bread on a cookie sheet in the oven. Turn the oven down to 325°F (165°C). Cut the bread into cubes. Combine the cubed bread and water in a large bowl. Fold in the crumbled feta cheese. Slowly add the moistened bread to the celery and onion mixture in the skillet, stirring constantly over low heat about 5 minutes to blend the flavors. Add additional margarine, if needed. Stir again. Turn into a casserole dish and garnish the top with roasted peppers and jalapeño slices, if desired. Cover and bake for 20 minutes. Uncover and continue baking until browned, about another 15 minutes.

[Variation: Crumbled, cooked chorizo *adds another spicy touch to this recipe. Mix 1½ cups of cooked and crumbled* chorizo *into the stuffing before turning the mixture into a casserole.]*

[Notita: Jars of preserved roasted red bell peppers are available in the Italian foods section of supermarkets.

MAKES 12 CUPS, OR ENOUGH FOR A 12 TO 14-POUND TURKEY OR PORK LOIN

Sauces & Spices

(Salsas y Especias)

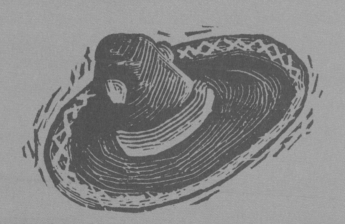

Sauces, or salsas, are either cooked or raw (*cruda*) in Mexican cuisine. "Salsa" refers not only to the bright red or green condiment you find on the table next to a basket of chips, but to more refined cooking sauces as well.

Cooked salsas are more subtle than the brilliant fresh sauces. Served warm or chilled, they keep better than the fresh sauces.

The red chile we use for red chile sauce is the Anaheim or long green chile that has ripened and then dried. It is the custom to tie red chiles in elongated bunches called *sartas* or *ristras* to take to market. In Tucson, the market often turns out to be a farmer's pickup truck parked on a vacant lot near an intersection on the city's outskirts. Sometimes sartas are used as a front door decoration or a kitchen decoration.

To prepare the basic red chile sauce, dried peppers are softened in boiling water, then ground into a rich, red paste. The paste is thinned with cooking liquid for use as a sauce for enchiladas and other dishes. Left thick and spiced with oregano and vinegar, it becomes *Salsa Adobada* (page 84) and is used as a marinade for *Carne* (beef) *Adobada* or *Puerco* (pork) *Adobado*.

Cherry Tomato, Mint, and Cucumber Salsa

This is a salsa *cruda*, meaning it is uncooked. It is bright and fresh, suitable for spooning onto almost any plate of food, from carne seca to poached salmon.

1	pint cherry tomatoes
1	pint yellow drop tomatoes (small tear-drop-shaped tomatoes)
2	cucumbers, peeled and diced in large chunks
1	teaspoon salt
1	teaspoon lemon pepper
1	tablespoon lemon juice
½	cup white onion, diced
½	cup green chiles, diced
1	teaspoon garlic, minced
¼	cup chile oil
2	tablespoons chile vinegar
1	cup chopped fresh mint
1	bunch mint leaves, for garnish

Wash the tomatoes and place in a glass bowl. Add the cucumbers, salt, lemon pepper, lemon juice, onion, garlic, oil, and vinegar. Gently mix and add the mint last. Refrigerate to let all the flavors blend. To make a perfect fresh salsa, do not over mix it, nor make it too much ahead of time. After 30 minutes place the mixture in a large bowl and garnish the edge of the bowl with fresh mint leaves and a splash of chile vinegar.

[Notita: Green chiles can be omitted, and fresh crunchy bell peppers of any color can be added to give additional zip to this salad. Or you can keep the chiles, and add the bell peppers also.]

MAKES ABOUT 8 CUPS

Escabeche
Vegetable Pickle

Many of the world's cuisines have a hot pickled-vegetable relish to spice up food that needs a jolt of flavor. Italians use *giardiniera;* at El Charro, it's *escabeche* (pickled vegetables). Carlotta likes to use the hot, vinegary potion as a garnish for any bland food as well as dressing for potato salad. "Use your favorite vegetables to marinate in the sauce," she says. "It's up to you."

½	cup lemon or lime juice
2	tablespoons canola oil
1	teaspoon garlic purée (page 93)
1	chipotle chile, minced
2	tablespoons rice vinegar, or white wine vinegar
1	bay leaf
½	tablespoon cayenne
2	large carrots, cut into 8 sticks
½	white onion, cut into rings
1	medium jicama, peeled, and cut into strips

Choose from a variety of other vegetables: cauliflower, turnip, cucumber, zucchini or other squash, garbanzo beans, kidney beans, string beans, etc.

To make the marinade, combine the juice, oil, garlic purée, chile, vinegar, bay leaf, and cayenne in a jar with a tight-fitting lid. Shake well. Place the cut vegetables in a nonreactive bowl, such as glass or stainless steel, and pour the marinade over them. Toss to coat. Cover with plastic wrap, and refrigerate several hours to blend the flavors.

MAKES 4 TO 6 SERVINGS

Green Chile Preparation

Chiles, especially the long green or Anaheim chiles, are usually prepared for cooking before they are incorporated into a recipe. In this book, you will be asked to prepare the chiles according to the following instructions.

The outer layer or skin of the chile and usually the seeds are removed before the chile is used. Cooks have devised several methods for doing this.

One method is to scorch the skin by holding the chile near a flame, such as under (or over) a gas broiler or stuck on a long fork held over the range-top burner. Others prefer to boil the chiles in oil until the skin loosens. Whichever way you choose, *¡cuidado!* Be careful! Never touch your eyes or mouth while you have chile oils on your hands. They are very potent. Wear plastic gloves if you find your skin is intolerant, and wash your hands well afterward.

Direct-flame method: Pierce chiles 2 or 3 times each with a fork and place them on your oven rack under the broiler. (Gas flames work better than electric burners.) Keep turning them until the chiles brown or blacken evenly. Immediately place them in a paper bag or covered pot and let them rest for about 20 minutes. When cool enough to handle, gently peel away most of the fragile, filmy skin, leaving the stem intact, if possible. The presence of the stem proves you are not serving canned chiles when you present *Chiles Rellenos* (page 62).

Boiling-oil method: Pierce each chile 2 or 3 times with a fork. Heat oil in a mini-fryer according to manufacturer's directions for French fries; or partially fill (about ⅓ of capacity) a deep, heavy saucepan with oil, and heat until the thermometer reaches the temperature marked for deep frying. Immerse the chiles, 2 or 3 at a time, into the oil until blisters form on the chiles. (The moisture in the chiles is considerable; expect much spattering while they are in the hot oil.) Immediately remove the chiles and submerge them in a bowl of cold water. When all the chiles are blistered and cooled, peel them.

Salsa de Mango
Mango Salsa

Carlotta sings of the mango: "It is one of the most luscious fruits in the world, green and rosy on the outside and brilliant orange inside [with a] sweet and slightly salty taste and creamy texture that is totally quenching when eaten raw out of hand." Carlotta appreciates the mango also because it marries so well with other fruits and vegetables, as in this salsa with tomatoes, onions, and chiles. As a chef, she recommends it as a companion to either chicken or pork. Her description of its taste? "Like nothing else in the world."

2	*mangos, or 1 jar mangos, peeled, diced, and puréed*
3	*tomatoes, chopped*
¼	*cup minced onion*
1	*tablespoon white vinegar*
1	*cup finely chopped fresh Anaheim chiles, roasted (page 79)*

Combine the mangos, tomatoes, onion, vinegar, and chiles in a glass bowl and blend well. Cover and chill.

[Notita: This salsa is perfect with chicken or pork.]

MAKES 6 TO 8 SERVINGS

Molé Poblano

This is a fairly new addition to our menu due to public demand. It is a specialty dish that is often associated with the Mexican-American holiday of Cinco de Mayo. Legend tells that there was a convent in Puebla. Since the French had been defeated in battle there, many dignitaries were visiting the convent at this time. Supplies were very limited, and the nuns invented *molé* (pasty sauce) from the various nuts and seeds that were in their pantry. Today, there are many commercial versions of jarred and powdered *molés* available. Or one can try one's hand with this recipe. Sometimes it is good to mix both versions together along with some homemade chicken broth to give the mole a richer taste. The difference between a *molé* and a sauce is that *molés* are thickened with seeds, herbs, and nuts, never a flour/roux base.

12	dried ancho chile peppers	1	teaspoon ground cinnamon
2¼	cups boiling water	1	teaspoon ground cloves
6	tablespoons almonds	1	teaspoon ground coriander
1	white onion, chopped	1	teaspoon salt
3	tablespoons garlic purée (page 93)	4	tablespoons oil
		3	cups chicken broth
2	tomatoes, chopped	2	ounces Mexican chocolate, cut into pieces
1	corn tortilla, fried in oil and broken into pieces		
3	tablespoons sesame seeds, toasted in heated pan for 10 to 15 seconds		

Soak the peppers in boiling water for 1 hour, or until soft. Drain, but retain the water. Discard the stems and seeds, and place the peppers in a blender. Add the almonds, onions, garlic, tomato, toasted tortilla pieces, cinnamon, cloves, coriander, salt, and ¼ cup of the chile water. Blend at medium speed. Add more chile water as needed, or until a paste is formed. Heat the oil in a pan, add the paste, and cook. Add the broth gradually and stir constantly. Add the chocolate until melted. If too thick, add more chile water. This is a heavy, thick, cream-texture sauce, and it is served over chicken or turkey. Sprinkle additional toasted sesame seeds over the *molé*.

MAKES 4 TO 6 SERVINGS

Pico de Charro
Chunky Green Chile and Tomato Sauce

Recalling childhood picnics in the Santa Catalina foothills with Monica, Carlotta says, "Monica's fresh green salsa was a work of art. The fresh green chiles were charred before peeling, giving them a woodsy aroma and a slightly softened texture. They were chopped and combined with vine-ripened garden tomatoes, garlic, and onion, a little vinegar and oil, pepper and salt. Monica added some succulent pinto beans and silken tortillas and we had a celebration of family and food."

2	cloves garlic, peeled
½	teaspoon salt
1	teaspoon vinegar
1	teaspoon oil
6	fresh Anaheim chiles, roasted (page 79) chopped
6	ripe tomatoes, chopped
1	medium white onion, chopped
½	teaspoon additional salt, or to taste
1	teaspoon ground black pepper
	Chopped cilantro (optional)

Mash the garlic in a small wooden salad bowl, using the ½ teaspoon salt as a grinding agent. Stir in the vinegar and oil. In a large glass bowl combine with the chiles, tomatoes, onion, additional salt if needed, black pepper, and cilantro, if using. Cover and chill for several hours before serving.

MAKES 2 CUPS

Salsa Adobo
Chile Paste

It is the starting place for many good-tasting recipes," Carlotta says of *Salsa Adobo*. "Thinned with a cooking liquid, such as chicken broth, it becomes a sauce for enchiladas and other dishes. Unthinned, with vinegar or herbs added, it is called *adobado*. Adobado is a wonderful marinade for beef or pork"

12	*dried red chiles*
2	*quarts boiling water*

Rinse the chiles in cold water and remove the stems. Cook in the boiling water until tender, about 15 minutes. Remove the chiles and reserve the cooking liquid.

Place a few of the chiles in a blender or food processor with ½ cup of the reserved liquid, and blend to a paste. Remove to a bowl. Repeat with the remaining chiles.

MAKES ABOUT 2 QUARTS

Mariachi Music

The mariachi-charro connection is a close one, so close that they look virtually alike. It did not begin that way. The original mariachi bands of the mid-nineteenth century were quartets from the southern part of Jalisco in west-central Mexico, dressed in humble peasant garb for their performances. Their music grew from a blend of European melody, African rhythm, and native Mexican tradition, all played out with great gusto on harps, guitars, and *vihuelas*. Mariachis sing of love, betrayal, and heroic deeds with great ardor and sometimes self-conscious humor (as in the famous mariachi song "La Cucaracha," about the cockroach).

The source of the name *mariachi* is curious. Some linguistic scholars say it is derived from a festival for a virgin known as Maria H. (*mah-ree-aa-heche*); others suspect it reflects a word from an extinct Coca Indian language of Jalisco that described the kind of wood used to build platforms on which village musicians performed.

After the Revolution of 1910, many mariachis had the wherewithal to outfit themselves in something flashier than the peasant clothes by which they were originally identified. By the teens, when Monica Flin married the dashing caballero who was her first husband, it was common for folkloric musical presentations to be about the colorful adventures of charros. These traveling shows included performances by mariachis whose sartorial inspiration was, like that of the charros themselves, the lavish outfits of Mexico's wealthiest landowners: tight-fitted pants with brocade ornamentation, short colorful coats with silver conchos and embroidery, and broad-brimmed sombreros.

In 1920 the well-known mariachi Cirilo Marmolejo moved from Jalisco to Mexico City, and three years later a cantina called Salón Tenampa opened on what is now Plaza Garibaldi. The Tenampa became the center of mariachi activity in Mexico City and began to attract groups from all over the countryside. When these groups came to the big city, any remaining peasant ways and peasant fashions were left behind.

At the time El Charro Café opened in 1922, it had become common for mariachi bands to wear flashy charro outfits. When the mariachi were proclaimed Mexico's official musical ensemble in the 1930s, their look had become indistinguishable from that of the charro. The first charro film in 1932, *Alla en el Rancho Grande*, featured a singing charro who could just as well have been a member of a mariachi band.

Mariachi music evolved dramatically in the twentieth century, adding trumpets and guitars to its typical battery of instruments. In 1971 Mariachi Cobre, a group from Tucson, became the first very successful Mexican-American mariachi ensemble. In 1988 Linda Ronstadt issued *Canciones de Mi Padre*, which contained mariachi

songs that were an homage to her own past. (Her family is as old and venerable a part of Tucson history as Monica Flin's.)

One of the biggest events of the year in Tucson (after the *charreada*/rodeo called Fiesta de los Vaqueros in February) is the Mariachi Festival in April. Described by *Tucson Weekly* as a "week-long confluence of music, dance, passion, and fire" (not to mention floor-splintering *zapatiado* dancing with hard-heeled boots), the event celebrates the roots and the evolution of mariachi music. Featuring mariachi bands from all over Mexico and the U.S. Southwest, the festival has frequently included performances by Linda Ronstadt, as well as Mariachi Vargas de Tecalitlan, the ensemble that has long been considered the premier artist of the genre.

Among the best-known mariachi songs are "La Cucaracha," "La Bamba," "Guantanamera," "El Rancho Grande," and "Besame Mucho."

Salsa para Tacos
Taco Sauce

Here is a very basic tomato sauce that is good not only for tacos, but also for spreading thin across flat tostadas and even as a dressing for a green salad. Carlotta points out that to most Mexicans, a taco is a snack food; in the U.S., we tend to think of them by twos and threes as a meal.

1	(16-ounce) can crushed tomatoes
1	cup canned tomato purée, or substitute ½ cup canned tomato paste mixed with ½ cup water
1	cup water
½	medium white onion, chopped
½	cup garlic purée (page 93)
½	cup oil
¼	cup vinegar
4	tablespoons dried leaf oregano
1	teaspoon salt, or to taste
4	de árbol chiles, crushed (optional)

Mix the tomatoes, tomato purée, water, onion, garlic purée, oil, vinegar, oregano, salt, and chiles in a saucepan. Bring to the boil and turn off the heat. Cool. Taste and adjust seasoning. Can be served hot or cold. Refrigerate up to one week.

MAKES 1 QUART

Salsa Verde para Enchiladas
Green Enchilada Sauce

A relatively complicated sauce that Carlotta uses to coat chicken breasts before baking them. Once they are baked, top the breasts with more of the sauce, some crumbly Mexican cheese (or feta) and chopped tomatoes. Return them to the oven until the sauce bubbles and serve them with crusty French bread rather than tortillas for soaking up maximum amounts of the sauce. To make a plate particularly attractive, sauce one part of the dish with green salsa and the other part with red.

2	tablespoons vegetable oil
½	white onion, chopped
2	tablespoons flour
2	cups chopped Anaheim chiles
¼	cup garlic purée (page 93)
2	cups chicken stock (or use bouillon cubes)
¾	teaspoon salt, or to taste

In a medium skillet heat the oil and sauté the onion. Add the flour and mix well. Stir in the chiles, garlic purée, stock, and salt and simmer for 20 minutes. Purée in a blender. Use immediately as a warm sauce for enchiladas or refrigerate or freeze for later use.

MAKES ABOUT 3 CUPS

El Charro Red Enchilada Sauce

This is El Charro's version of what is perhaps the most basic of all Mexican sauces, used not only in enchiladas but in countless other dishes. Although it is available in cans at the supermarket, canned sauce is *never* as good as that you make yourself from dried red chiles. "If you do nothing else from scratch, at least make your own enchilada sauce," Carlotta implores.

12	dried red chiles
2	quarts boiling water
3	tablespoons oil
¼	cup garlic purée, (page 93)
3	tablespoons flour
½	teaspoon salt, or to taste

Rinse the chiles in cold water and remove the stems. Cook in the boiling water until tender, about 15 minutes. Remove the chiles and reserve the cooking liquid. Place a few of the chiles in a blender or food processor with ½ cup of the reserved liquid, and blend to a paste. Remove to a bowl. Repeat with the remaining chiles.

Heat the oil in a large skillet. Add the garlic purée and flour, stirring until flour browns. Add the chile paste, stirring constantly until it boils and thickens. Season with the salt. Thin slightly with the cooking liquid.

MAKES 2 QUARTS

Bouquet Garni Embellishments

A bouquet garni is a ready-made "package" of favorite herbs to add to dishes while cooking. Just take a bunch of herbs (the classic trio is parsley, thyme, and bay leaf) and tie them together or place them in a cheesecloth bag. Tying or bagging the herbs allows for easy removal before the dish is served.

With these ready-made "bouquets," I can cut down on my scavenging time in the cupboards. I have definite herbs that I use most often in soups, stocks, and sauces, and they are fun to make and a great time saver in my busy day. Purchased herbs can be used for your bouquet garni—just make sure they are fresh. I never use dried parsley as I might with thyme or bay leaf; it is always much better to add fresh parsley or cilantro at the time of cooking. You can always tie the parsley or cilantro to the garni, and then fish it out at the end of cooking. Some of my chef friends will put coarsely crumbled herbs into cheesecloth squares and tie them with a string. No matter what the cook's method is, the results are always good.

Carlotta's Basic Garni
Start with a bay leaf and dried thyme and add garlic cloves at the time of cooking. Because I use so much garlic, I will often start with a purée and blend it with all my ingredients. This is just a personal choice, and each cook needs to determine the method that works for him or her.

For beef:
Add dried celery leaves. Often I will leave the celery tops in the oven at 200°F (95°C) until crisp and then add a fresh green chili tied to the bouquet to add zing.

For poultry:
Take the standard bouquet garni and add fresh leaves of tarragon or a bit of lemon thyme. If you have fresh carrots, add this to your bouquet.

For fish:
Fresh dill is always the best herb to use with fish. Fortunately, our produce departments always have it available. I like to make the bouquet and let it dry over my kitchen window. My cats enjoyed it so much that I had to change the drying spot, or I would end up with all my herbs in the sink and string on the counter.

Tomato sauces:
Add basil and oregano without the bay leaf. For Mexican chile sauces I leave out the basil and bay leaf but add the oregano and chives.

Other bouquets:
Dried onion, pickling spices, mustard seeds, cloves, and cinnamon — all of these ingredients can be tinkered with to make exciting and interesting flavors for standard dishes. Don't be afraid to experiment with other possibilities.

Garlic Purée

Whenever you see "garlic purée" in recipes in this book, the recipe calls for garlic prepared in the manner described here. If you use a lot of garlic, prepare a batch to be used within about a week's time. Don't store for too long as garlic spoils and can become toxic if stored in oil.

4	garlic bulbs
¼	cup water

Smash the garlic cloves with the side of a wide knife; the peels will slip off easily. Peel the garlic heads and put them in a blender with the water. Purée the garlic until it is the consistency of applesauce. Store the purée in a tightly sealed glass jar in the refrigerator, making sure to use it within 1 week.

MAKES ½ CUP

Hot Pepper Oil

Hot pepper oil is easy to make and keep on hand for adding to salads, as well as for stir-frying and a quick pick-me-up for pasta sauce.

2	cups canola oil
⅓	cup tiny, crushed hot red peppers, chiltepin or pequin

Place the oil and dried peppers in a saucepan. Heat until the fizzing stops, taking care not to let the mixture smoke. Let the oil/pepper mixture cool. Strain through a fine mesh sieve. Press the peppers to extract the oil. (Make sure you use gloves to protect your hands.) Funnel the oil into a dry bottle and add a dry whole red pepper for appearance and to denote its spicy flavor. Store in a cool place, or refrigerate. Cloudiness of refrigerated oil is harmless; just bring to room temperature and shake.

MAKES 2 CUPS

Infused Hot Pepper Vinegar

This is an excellent sprinkle for enchiladas or salads. (It takes about 2 weeks to prepare.)

12	fresh green peppers, green, red, or yellow
1	ounce dried red peppers, chiltepin or pequin
3	cups distilled white vinegar

Rinse and dry the peppers (make sure to wear gloves to protect your hands as these are very hot peppers). Stem and chop the peppers into medium coarse pieces. Place the peppers in a clean, heatproof, quart jar with a tight fitting lid. Heat the vinegar to simmering and pour over the peppers. Uncover and cool the mixture, then recap and tighten the lid. Let the mixture stand for two weeks while shaking occasionally. Taste with caution.

Strain the mixture through a fine mesh strainer. Press the debris of peppers to extract the flavor. Bottle the liquid in a clean dry bottle and cap tightly. You can add whole red peppers to the bottle for appearance and to add to the spicy flavor.

MAKES 3 CUPS

Strawberry Vinegar

This is a very delicate flavor that enhances any fruit-based salsa. It takes about one month to ripen.

2	quarts ripe strawberries
4	cups white wine vinegar or rice vinegar
8	tablespoons sugar

Sort the strawberries, remove the stems, rinse, and drain. Crush or chop the berries and combine them with the vinegar in a sterilized, two-quart jar. Cover the jar and let the berries sit for one month. Shake at least once every two days. At the end of the month, empty the mixture into a fine-meshed sieve lined with a cheesecloth and set over a bowl. Let the vinegar drain; press lightly on solid debris to obtain all juice. Discard the pulp. Combine the sugar and vinegar in a stainless saucepan and heat uncovered to simmering for 4 minutes. Let the mixture cool completely. Skim off the foam and strain into one or two sterilized bottles. Cap the bottles and store in a cool place. If sediment appears, filter the juice through a paper coffee filter.

MAKES ABOUT 2 QUARTS

Cinco de Mayo

Cinco de Mayo (5th of May) commemorates the victory of a ragtag band of Mexican soldiers led by General Porfirio Diaz over the French at the Battle of Puebla in 1862. Puebla is an especially important place in the history of Mexican food, for it is said that *molé* was invented here. The legend is that a group of local nuns wanted to make a special meal for a bishop traveling through town. But they had no deluxe groceries. Using their minimal store of seeds and herbs, they concocted the rich spicy sauce called *molé* that is now a vital part of the Mexican kitchen, frequently served as part of a traditional *Cinco de Mayo* menu.

"The holiday doesn't mean much anymore to those of us who are fifth- and sixth-generation Tucsonans," Carlotta Flores has commented. "But I learned to celebrate it with Monica. Monica celebrated everything she possibly could, especially May 4, the day before *Cinco de Mayo* and the birthday of the saint for which she was named."

Carlotta's reminiscences of Monica's Saint's Day celebrations in May are of outdoor picnics. "The cars were packed, and so was the feast. Forget sandwiches! This was a picnic of such delicious food that I get hungry thinking about it even after all these years. There was fried chicken, but not ordinary fried chicken. This had been drenched in garlic and vinaigrette dressing, rolled in seasoned flour, and then fried. We took along green corn tamales, Mexican potato salad, and *salsa de chile verde*. Monica added succulent pinto beans and tortillas, and we had a celebration of family and food.

"Some of us piled into my dad's and uncles' cars, but Monica traveled in her black 1952 Ford—the very latest model. Uncle

Steve drove with '*Tía Mamie*' and the feast in the back seat. We all followed to the picturesque and cool Sabino Canyon in the Santa Catalina Mountain foothills. Later in the day, satisfied with wonderful food and serenaded by the running stream, we napped in the shade of mesquite trees."

While most of the family dressed casually for the picnic, Monica had her own way about her. "She loved clothes," Carlotta says. "She was especially crazy about hats. Wherever Monica went, even on picnics, she dressed with style and wore one of her famous hats."

Pico de Gallo
A Seasoning Mix

Pico de Gallo means "bite from the rooster's beak"; and this seasoning mixture of chile, salt, and peppers does have a delicious smack! When it is sprinkled on a bouquet of fresh fruit, it amplifies the fruit's sweetness and gives the tongue a mouth-watering mixed message of spiced heat and cool refreshment. About the only fruit that Carlotta recommends *not* sprinkling with *Pico de Gallo* is strawberries. Otherwise, try it on peaches, plums, pears, oranges, kiwi, watermelon, grapefruit, grapes, jicama, mango, and coconut. And to even further gild the lily, you might want to also add a spritz of lime juice, a bit of crumbled queso fresco, or a sprinkling of toasted pecans.

3	*tablespoons paprika*
1	*tablespoon cayenne*
1	*tablespoon finely ground black pepper*
1	*tablespoon salt (decrease as desired)*
2	*tablespoons ground red chile*

Mix together and store in a shaker on your spice shelf.

Salads

(Ensaladas)

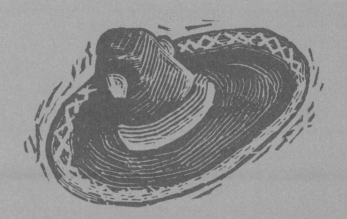

El Charro's best-known salad, the *Topopo a la Jalisciense* (pages 108–109) is a mighty meal unto itself, and Carlotta's health consciousness has inspired her to create all sorts of salads to precede or accompany an El Charro meal. To the home cook, she offers this low-fat *notita*: "Buy a small spray bottle and fill it with your favorite salad oil. When assembling your salad greens, spray them lightly with the oil and toss. You'll be amazed at how little oil is used. Then dress the salad with dressing made without additional oil."

Ceviche
Seafood Salad

At El Charro, the seafood for *Ceviche* is blanched before marinated, but the real cooking is done by the action of the citrus marinade. Carlotta's suggestion for a low-calorie *Ceviche* is to make it without the oil. She also advocates adding small pieces of mango, orange, or apple as a sweet balance to the pungent marinade.

MARINADE:

12	Anaheim chiles, roasted (page 79) chopped
½	cup chopped green onion
¼	cup garlic purée (page 93)
1	cup chopped celery
2	tablespoons hot sauce
1	tablespoon salt
1	tablespoon ground black pepper
1	cup chopped cilantro
4	tablespoons canned capers
1	cup fresh lime juice
¼	cup white vinegar
½	cup oil
¼	cup chopped red onion
1	avocado, pitted, peeled, chopped
2	pounds firm seafood (monkfish, cod, red snapper, scallops, or a combination)
1	quart boiling water

GARNISH:

2	ripe avocados, seeded, peeled, and chopped
8	thin slices lime
8	celery ribs, cut into sticks

Several hours before serving, combine the chiles, green onions, garlic purée, celery, hot sauce, salt, pepper, cilantro, capers, lime juice, vinegar, oil, red onion, and avocado in a nonreactive bowl. Next, cut the seafood into ½-inch cubes, and blanch in boiling water a few seconds. Drain; then carefully layer the fish or seafood in a ceramic bowl alternately with the marinade. Cover with plastic wrap, and refrigerate immediately. Let marinate until the fish loses its translucency (at least 4 hours), stirring gently after 2 hours and again before serving. To serve, spoon mixture into cocktail glasses, and garnish with chopped avocado, lime slices, and celery sticks.

MAKES 6 TO 8 SERVINGS

Cilantro and Green Cabbage Slaw

Cabbage is a very popular dish in Mexican food. It is used in many instances over lettuce, especially in soft tortilla taquitos. It is especially wonderful when the following dressing is added to the cabbage. (It can also be used with enchiladas.)

DRESSING:

½	cup oil
⅓	cup lime juice
1	tablespoon vinegar
¼	cup garlic purée (page 93) or two minced garlic cloves
1	teaspoon salt
1	teaspoon lemon pepper

SLAW:

1	head green cabbage, finely shredded
¼	cup minced cilantro
	Dressing (ingredients above)
¼	cup diced green onion
1	cucumber, peeled and diced for garnish
2	limes, cut in wedges
4	radishes, cut in slices
2	tablespoon dried chile flakes (optional)

To make the dressing combine the oil, lime juice, vinegar, garlic, salt, and lemon pepper in a jar with a tight lid. Shake well to mix.

For the salad, in a large bowl mix the cabbage and cilantro and toss with the dressing. You can mix in the green onion, cucumbers, limes, and radishes, or serve them platter style (so picky eaters can choose their veggies). Sprinkle with the chile flakes, if using. If you do not mix all the ingredients together, you can add shredded *cojita* or any other white cheese to this salad for added panache, and, of course, your favorite salsa is already part of this selected side dish.

[Notita: Dressing can be made in advance and kept up to two days in the refrigerator. Store in a glass jar.]

MAKES 6 TO 8 SERVINGS

Ensalada de Camaron con Tequila
Shrimp Salad with Tequila

Like the spices in a traditional red cocktail sauce, tequila has a vibrancy that brings out the best in firm-fleshed shrimp.

½	cup chile oil
2	teaspoons crushed red pepper flakes
1	teaspoon salt
1	teaspoon lemon pepper
¼	cup diced green onion
¼	cup chopped parsley
¼	cup finely diced cilantro
¼	cup lime juice
1	fresh jalapeño, finely chopped, stemmed, and seeded
½	cup tequila
2	tablespoons triple sec
1	pound medium shrimp (16 to 20 count) cooked, cleaned, and deveined
2	avocados, diced and tossed in ½ cup lime juice
3	cups baby spinach
3	cups romaine lettuce
1	cup diced tomato
1	cup diced cucumber
½	dozen tortilla strips (tossed and fried with cotija cheese, see page 113)
2	limes, cut into wedges for garnish

Place the oil, pepper flakes, salt, lemon pepper, green onion, parsley, cilantro, lime juice, jalapeño, tequila, and triple sec into a glass bowl. Add the shrimp, toss, cover with plastic wrap, and set aside. In a separate bowl mix the avocados, spinach, romaine, tomato, and cucumber in a large bowl and toss with half of the shrimp mixture. Add some of the tortilla strips in the middle and surround the salad with the remaining shrimp. Garnish with the limes.

MAKES 4 SERVINGS

The Virgin of Guadalupe

People always give me religious icons, especially the Virgin de Guadalupe," says Carlotta Flores. Images of the Virgin of Guadalupe abound in the restaurant. Among the many saints whose pictures are reproduced over and over in Southwestern culture, none is more popular than the virgin. According to Jim Griffith in his wonderful book *Saints of the Southwest, Nuestra Señora de Guadalupe* the virgin appears as a picture or statue in such expected places as churches and home altars, but also as an image on silkscreened T-shirts and low-rider cars. Her likeness will be found at political rallies and union marches. She has truly transcended her role as a religious figure to become the Virgin of the Americas, a symbol of Mexican identity.

As can be seen at El Charro, most images of the Virgin of Guadalupe show her with roses at her feet. This depiction dates back to the 1500s, when a man named Juan Diego was walking in Mexico and saw an apparition of the Virgin Mary. The Virgin told the humble man to go to the Bishop of Mexico City, which he did twice. But each time, he was rebuffed. On the third trip, the Virgin instructed Juan Diego to bring wild roses. He found these roses growing at the exact spot where she appeared, and he brought them to the Bishop. The Bishop saw that an image of the Virgin

Mary was imprinted on Juan Diego's cloak, the cloak in which he had wrapped the roses.

The rose vines that creep up the outside walls of El Charro have been known to mysteriously bloom on December 12, the Virgin's feast day. On our last trip to El Charro, Jane bought a wonderful pair of Mexican earrings made of recycled bottle caps decorated with sequins and the image of the Virgin. And while the virgin lives on as an image in religious and popular culture, Juan Diego is soon to be canonized as a saint.

Ensalada de Elote
Corn Salad

Carlotta suggests that this recipe can be made with either canned or frozen corn or, for that matter, fresh corn kernels carefully scraped off the cob. She also advises that this recipe invites improvisation in the form of added garbanzos or kidney beans, or even the pickled vegetable relish known as *escabeche* (page 78).

1	quart water
2	(16-ounce) packages frozen yellow corn
1	teaspoon salt, or to taste
¾	cup Basic Vinaigrette (pages 108–109)
1	(8-ounce) can pimientos, drained and minced
1	(4-ounce) jar jalapeños, drained and minced
1	cup chopped fresh cilantro
1	teaspoon salt, or to taste
2	fresh tomatoes, minced
1	red onion, minced

Cook the corn according to package instructions; set aside to cool. In a ceramic bowl, toss the corn with the Basic Vinaigrette and the pimientos, jalapeños, cilantro, salt, tomatoes, and red onion. Cover with plastic wrap and refrigerate 2 hours. Serve chilled as a vegetable dish or relish.

MAKES 6 TO 8 SERVINGS

Ensalada de Nopales
Prickly Pear Salad

Eating cactus is second nature to long-time Tucsonans. Prickly pear pads are gathered from private gardens in the spring (wild cacti are protected from poachers) or purchased already de-thorned in markets. To prepare a fresh-picked cactus pad requires some expertise as well as thick gardening gloves to prevent getting stuck by thorns), but the good news is that prickly pear salad can be made from well-rinsed, canned *nopalitos*, which are available in markets that specialize in southwestern produce.

12	prickly-pear pads (nopales, nopalitos), cut into strips
6	tomatoes, chopped
1	large onion, chopped
4	jalapeños, chopped
½	cup chopped cilantro, optional
2	tablespoons vinegar

Cook the cactus pads in water to remove the slippery gel. When tender, rinse the pads in cold water, and chop. In a glass or ceramic bowl, combine the chopped nopales with the tomatoes, onion, jalapeños, cilantro, and vinegar. Serve immediately on lettuce leaves, or cover and chill to enable flavors to become bolder.

[Notita: Serve Ensalada de Nopales scrambled into eggs or as a relish or side dish.]

MAKES 6 SERVINGS

Topopo a la Jalisciense
Volcano Salad Jalisco-style

Topopo is an Indian word for volcano, and that is what it looks like: a conical monument of shredded lettuce and marinated vegetables with columns of cheese, carrots, and celery running down the outside, a wheel of tomato strewn with olive chunks on top, all resting on a foundation of a tostada and shredded chicken or carne seca. It is a festival of textures and tastes, a dazzling sight, and a fortifying meal. Many restaurants around Tucson now serve their own version of the *topopo* salad, but there is little doubt that Monica Flin is the one who invented it. Family history says that she was inspired to create the monumental meal after gazing upon the volcano Popocatépetl outside Mexico City. And Carlotta surmises that she named it *Topopo a la Jalisciense* because Topopo Popocatépetl is just too hard to say.

Basic Vinaigrette:

½	cup oil
¼	cup white vinegar
	salt and pepper

SALAD:

	Oil for frying
8	corn tortillas
2	cups Frijoles Refritos (page 67)
4	small romaine lettuce heads, julienned
2	cups frozen mixed vegetables, cooked
	Salt
	Pepper
1	cup Basic Vinaigrette
4	boneless chicken breasts, poached, skinned, each cut into 8 strips
2	large avocados, sliced into 16 pieces
32	strips Jack cheese
1	(7-ounce) jar jalapeños, drained, sliced
2	tomatoes, quartered
8	green olives, chopped
1	cup shredded Mexican cheese

To make the Basic Vinaigrette, shake the oil, vinegar, and salt and pepper to taste in a covered jar, or slowly whisk the oil into the vinegar and seasons.

[Variation: Some cooks like to add a dash of sugar and a dab of strong mustard to this dressing.]

[Low-fat notita: Buy a small spray bottle and fill it with your favorite salad oil. When assembling your salad greens, spray them lightly with the oil and toss. You'll be amazed at how little oil is used. Then dress the salad with a dressing made without additional oil.]

In a large skillet heat the oil and fry the tortillas for a few seconds; set aside to drain on paper towels. In a saucepan heat the Frijoles Refritos, cover, and keep warm. In a bowl combine the lettuce with the cooked vegetables and salt and pepper to taste. Moisten with the Basic Vinaigrette.

To serve each salad, spread ¼ cup Frijoles Refritos on each fried tortilla. Pack 2 cups of the salad mixture into a 4-inch funnel and unmold it onto the prepared tortilla. Garnish with one-eighth of the chicken, avocado, cheese strips, and jalapeños placed vertically along the slopes of the volcano. At the summit of the Topopo, place one tomato quarter and then sprinkle with the chopped olives and cheese. Serve with additional Basic Vinaigrette on the side.

[Variation 1: Lately I find our guests enjoy a choice of dressings, including a vinaigrette made with raspberry vinegar or prickly-pear-flavored vinegar.]

[Variation 2: This versatile salad can be made with cooked whole pinto beans or guacamole on the bottom.]

MAKES 8 SERVINGS

Ensalada de Pasta con Pollo y Salsa de Tequila
Chicken Pasta Salad with Tequila

Everyone has a pasta salad favorite; we like this one because the colors add to the festive idea of having a salad dressing with tequila.

DRESSING:

½   cup chile oil

¼   cup chile vinegar

½   cup sour cream

2   tablespoons lime juice

1   cup diced green chiles

1   cup orange juice

1   teaspoon salt

1   teaspoon pepper

¼   cup garlic purée (page 93) or 1 teaspoon minced garlic

½   cup white tequila

PASTA AND CHICKEN:

4   cups cooked cheese tortellini

1   pound boned, cooked chicken breast, cut in cubes or fajita slices

½   cup green olives with pimientos

1   (12-ounce) can Mexicorn, drained

1   (16-ounce) can black beans, rinsed and drained

1   (16-ounce) can red kidney beans, rinsed and drained

1   (16-ounce) can white beans, (Great Northern or Cannellini) rinsed and drained

1   cup cooked, cooled, and diced green squash

1   cup diced celery

¼   cup chopped parsley/cilantro mixture, for garnish

To make the dressing, combine the oil, vinegar, sour cream, lime juice, green chiles, orange juice, salt, pepper, garlic, and tequila in a blender or a clean jar with a tight lid and mix the ingredients well.

Cook the pasta as directed and drain. Coat the bottom of a large bowl with the dressing, and add the pasta. Toss the pasta with three-fourths of the dressing. In another large bowl begin to layer the pasta, chicken, pimiento, Mexicorn, black beans, kidney beans, white beans, squash, and celery. After all is layered, drizzle with the remaining one-fourth of the dressing and garnish with the parsley/cilantro mix. Cover with plastic wrap. Chill until ready to serve.

MAKES 10 TO 12 SERVINGS

Lent at El Charro

There is an unbreakable, inescapable link between the religious calendar and food," Carlotta Flores notes, pointing out traditions that range from *Rosca de Reyes* ("Three Kings Bread") served for the Feast of the Epiphany in January to Christmastime tamale parties. Of the many memories Carlotta Flores has of Lent, one of her favorites is of Monica's *Tacos de Camarón*—shrimp tacos.

El Charro continues to respect the tradition of meatless Lent by offering *Pescado Viscayena* (p. 120) every Friday, along with *Quelites* (p. 69), which is simply whole pinto beans (cooked without pork, of course) mixed with steamed spinach. These are accompanied by El Charro Rice (p. 55), an *Enchilada Sonoreses* (p. 23), and

Capirotada (p. 158) for dessert. On Good Friday, no music is played in the restaurant until after 5 P.M.

"It is important for us to display for guests and educate our staff about the culture and traditions of the family," Carlotta says. She recalls that when she was a child, when meat was forbidden during Lent, her sacrifice, like that of many children, was to give up chewing gum. "Many subtle changes were made around us," she remembers. "The church's holy water fonts were dry; small pebbles

111

were placed in the fonts to remind us of our place on earth; the Holy statues were covered with purple cloths to remind us that the church was in mourning. We learned to prepare leg of spring lamb, make hot cross buns, and dye Easter eggs, blending the diversity of the culture in our family through food and religion."

That diversity of culture includes not only Monica's well-traveled perspective, but French and Spanish great-uncles who were bakers, and Carlotta's Irish father and Arizona mother, as well as the local legacies of Native American and Mexican cuisine. That is why the Mexican restaurant El Charro offers such varied culinary

expressions as three-color flag cookies on Mexican Independence Day (September 16), thirteen wishes expressed by popping thirteen grapes at New Year's (a Latin American custom, see page 127), green corn tamales for St. Patrick's Day, piñatas and Mexican Popsicles for *Cinco de Mayo*, and vermicelli soup (*Sopa Seca de Fideo*, page 52) throughout the year.

Totopos y Totopitos
Corn Chips and Strips

Corn chips and strips are good for snacking, or as garnishes for soup or salad. Carlotta advises that a good low-fat alternative to the traditional fried *totopos* are baked chips. These are made by cutting the tortillas to the desired shape and baking them on a cookie sheet in the oven at 350°F for about 8 minutes or until they begin to brown. Turn over the pieces and continue baking until they are crisp. Remove them from the oven and sprinkle with salt. Serve immediately.

2	cups vegetable oil
12	corn tortillas

Heat the oil in a heavy, 7-inch skillet or saucepan. Cut the corn tortillas with scissors to desired shapes, and fry them briefly in hot oil, a few at a time. Drain them on a paper towel, cool, and bag. Use within a day or two.

Carlotta's Ensalada de Espinaca
Spinach Salad

Sweet, spicy, luxurious, and refreshing, Carlotta's spinach salad is crowned with toasted pecans. The fresher-toasted, the better.

6	navel oranges or tangerines, peeled, sectioned
1	cup seedless green grapes
4	avocados, pitted, peeled, cubed
1	red onion, sliced into thin rings
2	tablespoons vegetable, olive, or walnut oil
2	bunches fresh spinach
1	cup chopped, toasted pecans
1	cup crumbled Mexican cheese
	Balsamic vinegar
	Pico de Gallo seasoning (page 98)

In a large bowl gently toss the oranges, grapes, avocado cubes, and onion rings with the oil. Place the spinach on individual plates or salad bowls. Spoon the fruit mixture onto the spinach. Top each with the pecans and cheese. Pass the balsamic vinegar and a shaker of *Pico de Gallo* seasoning.

[Notita: To toast pecans or other nuts, place them in a large, hot, dry skillet and, constantly stirring or shaking the pan, cook until browned lightly, or spread the nuts on a cookie sheet and bake at 350°F (175°C) for 10 to 15 minutes. Toasting brings out the flavor and makes the nuts crispy. Spread on toweling to cool. May be toasted in advance and stored in an airtight container in the refrigerator.]

[Notita: Keep all nuts cold, even frozen, to keep them from spoiling.]

MAKES 12 SERVINGS

Ensalada de Noche Buena
Christmas Eve Salad

A celebration of winter fruits, this festive salad is often served inside hollowed-out orange halves with a sprinkle of coconut on top. Carlotta's low-fat version eliminates the cheese and coconut and lowers the amount of vinaigrette and toasted walnuts.

8	green apples
8	red apples
12	navel oranges
2	pomegranates
½	cup lemon juice
1	red onion, thinly sliced
1	green bell pepper, diced
¾	cup Basic Vinaigrette (pages 108–109)

GARNISH:

1	cup walnut pieces
1	cup cubed Jack cheese or Mexican cheese
1	cup seedless grapes
	Shredded coconut (optional)

Wash, core, and cube the apples. Peel and cube the oranges. (If you wish, cut the oranges in half on their equator, run a sharp knife around the flesh to remove it and save the empty halves to be used as serving shells for the salad.) Peel and separate the pomegranate sections. In a ceramic bowl combine the prepared fruit with the lemon juice, onion, and bell pepper. Toss with Basic Vinaigrette. Cover with plastic wrap, and set aside for 1 hour.

To serve, garnish with the grapes, cheese cubes, walnuts, additional dressing, and a sprinkling of coconut, if desired.

[Notita: The dressing for this salad can be made with infusions of vinegar with garlic or basil, or by adding a squeeze of lemon juice and just a dash of oil instead of the Basic Vinaigrette.]

[Notita: Infusions are made by steeping garlic, basil, other herbs, or spices in hot vinegar. Tea is an infusion made with hot water.]

[Low-fat notita: If you want to lower the fat and calories in the recipe, eliminate, or reduce, the amount of cheese, vinaigrette, walnut, and coconut.]

MAKES 8 TO 12 SERVINGS

Plato de Fruta
Fruit Platter

Until recently, sumptuous desserts were never a big part of the El Charro dining experience. Instead, it was customary to serve plates of seasonal fruit—a common sight on the tables of restaurants in Mexico City and Mazatlán. Carlotta recommends this same dish as a great way to start the day along with a sweet roll and a cup of dark coffee.

2	*mangos*
1	*pineapple*
½	*medium Juan Canary, cantaloupe, or honeydew melon*
4	*nectarines*
4	*tablespoons grated or flaked coconut*
2	*tablespoons chopped pecans*
	Pico de Gallo seasoning (page 98)
16	*to 24 Bing cherries*
2	*limes*

Slice through the pineapple lengthwise, including the leaves, if possible. (Otherwise, cut the leaves off and, if they look good, use them to garnish the plate.) Cut lengthwise once again, so you have four pieces, and again for eight pieces. Cut out the core section from each piece, and discard. Carefully slide a sharp knife under the flesh, about one-half inch from the pineapple shell, and remove it in one piece if possible, leaving the shell intact to be used as a "boat" bowl. Cut the pineapple into bite-size pieces. Prepare the remaining fruit as desired: Peel the melon, and cut it into chunks or balls; slice the nectarines, peeled or unpeeled. Arrange the fruit in and around the pineapple boats, and sprinkle with the coconut, nuts, and a dash of Pico de Gallo seasoning mix. Garnish with cherries and lime wedges.

MAKES 4 TO 8 SERVINGS

Founder Monica Flin and her three sisters Frances, Louisa, and Lydia Flin

Monica Flin in front of El Charro Café in the 1940s

Portrait of El Charro Café
employees in 1940

Like the Spanish bullfighters and the
United States' cowboys, the charro is a
national symbol in Mexico. The charro's
combination of horsemanship, derring-do,
chilvalry, noble purpose, and spectacular
wardrobe is expressed throughout El
Charro Café.

El Charro

Marion Olin   140 W. BROADWAY
                               TUCSON, ARIZONA

El Charro Café has a lot of Mexican memorabilia, including sombreros (left), and murals (above).

The front of El Charro Café as seen today

El Charro Café patio

El Charro Café serves authentic Tucson–Mexican food, including such delicious vegetarian recipes as Chile Rellenos and Calabacitas.

Some favorite dishes at El Charro Café include Tamales de Carne and fresh Chile con Carne served along the Famous Carne Seca . . . and of course, an ice cold cerveza!

Chile peppers aren't really peppers at all. To botanists they are berries, growers consider them fruit, and chefs think of them as a vegetable.

While Tucson's Mexican fare is rarely four-alarm hot as in neighboring New Mexico, the flavor of chile is fundamental.

El Charro and Sonoran culture is seen in the details throughout the restaurant from the colorful presentation of the food to the beautiful stained glass window.

Other than its food, probably the best-known thing about El Charro is its calendar. The images on the calendars include the especially popular Virgin of Guadalupe and couples courting, as depicted here.

Most images of the Virgin of Guadalupe show her with roses at her feet.

Festivals are an integral part of Mexican culture. The festive bone men, called *Muertos* or *Calaveros*, are a salute to the Mexican festival known as the Day of the Dead, a religious holiday celebrating the lives of those no longer with us. Another one is the Mariachi Festival that includes music and dancing to celebrate the roots and evolution of mariachi music.

Since 1922 El Charro Café has been feeding Tucson. Pictured to the left are Monica Flin and Grace Montano in 1945 with the Anheuser-Busch horses. And today (below) El Charro Café is a fixture of Tucson.

We are not the best because we're the oldest. We are the oldest because we're the best.

Fish, Chicken & Beef

(Pescado, Pollo y Carnes)

When it comes to cooking meat, Carlotta advises, "Paint with sauces; tune with spices." She describes the variations of meat filling for tacos, tamales, burritos, and sandwiches "like the paint strokes on a canvas" and says that "basically any cut of beef or pork, goat, chicken, or turkey can be slowly simmered in liquid and cut or pulled apart, producing an important component of Mexican food: shredded meat."

Pescado en Estilo de Enchilada
Baked Cod, Enchilada Style

Serving fish enchilada-style saves those of delicate sensibility from having to face an actual fish-shaped fish on their plate. Carlotta hints that making fish this way is a good technique for encouraging finicky children to learn to enjoy it. She also suggests that the dish is extra-special if garnished with garlicky grilled shrimp.

6	(6-ounce) pieces boneless cod, sea bass, or other firm, thick, white fish	2	cups yellow corn (optional)
¼	cup margarine	18	medium shrimp, shelled and deveined
1	tablespoon garlic purée (page 93)		**SAUCE:**
2	cups grated Monterey Jack cheese	½	cup garlic purée (page 93)
2	cups grated sharp Cheddar cheese	3	to 4 cups Enchilada Sauce (page 90) heated
2	cups Anaheim chile, roasted (page 79) chopped		**GARNISH:**
½	cup chopped green onion	1	cup crumbled, Mexican-style cheese
		½	cup chopped cilantro
		2	or 3 limes, cut into wedges
		2	or 3 oranges, cut into wedges

Preheat the oven to 350°F (175°C). In a lightly greased baking pan, place the fish in one layer. Combine the margarine with the garlic purée. Dot each piece using half of the garlic mixture, reserving the remainder. Cover loosely with foil. Bake in the oven about 15 minutes, until the fish is no longer translucent. Meanwhile in a large bowl combine the grated cheese, chiles, green onion, and corn, if using. Drain the juices from the partially cooked fish, and reserve. Top each piece of fish generously with the cheese mixture. Return to the pan, cover, and bake about 10 minutes until the cheese melts. In a large skillet, sauté the shrimp in the remaining garlic margarine until warmed through and just cooked.

To serve, heat a serving platter. In a sauce pan, heat the garlic purée, Enchilada Sauce, and reserved fish juices. Spoon some of the sauce onto the heated platter to coat it. Carefully transfer the fish and topping to the platter. Top with the shrimp, Mexican cheese, cilantro, and wedges of lime and orange.

MAKES 6 SERVINGS

Pescado Viscayena
Fish Fillets with Vegetables

Many Mexican menus offer a version of seafood Vera Cruz, to which Pescado Viscayena is very similar, minus the capers. This is the centerpiece of the traditional Lenten meal at El Charro, hearkening back to a time when it was mandatory to substitute fish for meat.

8	(6-ounce) boneless fish fillets (cod, sole, or snapper)
½	cup margarine, melted
	Salt and pepper
¼	cup fresh lime juice
1	white onion, sliced into rings

SAUCE:

¼	cup oil
2	green bell peppers, seeded, sliced into rings
2	or 3 potatoes, cooked, peeled, and diced
¼	cup lime juice

1	cup frozen peas and carrots
½	teaspoon hot sauce
½	cup chopped white onion
2	tablespoons garlic purée (page 93)
	Salt and pepper
½	cup fresh cilantro
6	Anaheim chiles, roasted (page 79) chopped
¼	cup water or white wine

GARNISH:

	Fresh cilantro
8	pieces lime

Preheat the oven to 325°F (165°C). Rinse and pat the fillets dry. Coat a glass baking pan with the melted margarine. Arrange the fillets in one layer in the pan. Sprinkle with salt and pepper to taste and lime juice and scatter the onion over all. Cover and bake in the oven 10 to 15 minutes, depending upon the thickness of the fish pieces. Drain off the broth, and reserve to add to the sauce just before serving.

To make the sauce, assemble and prepare the sauce ingredients while the fillets are baking. Fifteen minutes before serving, combine the oil, peppers, potatoes, lime juice, peas and carrots, Tabasco, onion, garlic purée, salt and pepper, cilantro, chiles, and water or wine in a large skillet and bring the mixture to the boil. Cover and simmer 10 minutes. Stir in the reserved fish broth. Spoon the sauce over the fillets and return them to the oven to finish cooking, about 10 minutes. Serve with the cilantro and lime garnish.

MAKES 8 SERVINGS

Shrimp Doblado

This recipe will stuff six enchiladas, or can be a main course with rice and a salad.

1	pound medium shrimp
½	stick (4 tablespoons) butter or margarine
1	medium yellow onion, chopped
⅓	cup garlic purée (page 93)
1	(16-ounce) can stewed tomatoes
½	cup chopped green peppers
½	cup chopped red peppers
6	green chiles (If using fresh, see directions for skinning. If using canned, be sure to rinse to avoid vinegar taste.)
	Lemon pepper
	Seasoning salt
	Black pepper

Add a fresh bay leaf to the broth. Drain the broth and use it as a base for the stuffing. In a large skillet melt the butter or margarine. Add the onion, garlic purée, tomatoes, peppers, chiles, lemon pepper, seasoning salt, and black pepper to taste. Simmer for 20 minutes. Add the shrimp last and make sure not to overcook, since they will become tough.

MAKES 6 SERVINGS

Salmón con Salsa de Cilantro Pesto
Salmon with Cilantro Pesto Sauce

Cilantro was not a part of the El Charro kitchen's repertoire until fairly recently. Carlotta attributes its popularity in modern Mexican cooking partly to the spread of California-Mex cuisine as well as to the influence of Asian chefs. "It may be one of those culturally exchanged delights that came about as Mexico was populated by peoples from all over the world."

4	pounds large, skinned salmon fillets
¼	plus ¾ cup lime juice
1	cup chopped green onions, including tops
2	pickled jalapeño chiles, finely chopped
1½	cups fresh, finely chopped cilantro
½	cup pine nuts plus about 1 tablespoon for garnish
½	cup olive oil
½	cup melted margarine
10	lime wedges

Preheat the oven to 350°F (175°C). Place the fillets in a baking dish. Drizzle the ¼ cup lime juice over the fillets. In a mixing bowl combine the remaining ¾ cup lime juice, green onions, chiles, cilantro, pine nuts, and olive oil. Spread ½ cup of the mixture over the center of the fish. Bake until the fish is translucent, about 40 minutes. Remove the fish with a slotted spatula. Drizzle the melted margarine on the fish and spoon the remaining salsa down the center of the fish fillets. Garnish with the tablespoon or more of the pine nuts and the lime wedges.

MAKES 6 TO 8 SERVINGS

Tacos de Camarón
Shrimp Tacos

Some of Carlotta's most delicious memories are of the shrimp tacos that Monica served during Lent. On the side of the tacos was macaroni salad; and for dessert: lime sherbet.

1	tablespoon butter or margarine
½	onion, minced
3	jalapeños, chopped
2	tomatoes, chopped
¼	teaspoon garlic purée (page 93)
	Pepper
1	pound boiled shrimp, shelled, deveined, and roughly chopped (or use small shrimp)
	Juice of 1 lemon
	Juice of 2 limes
12	corn tortillas, folded in half and lightly deep fried
3	cups (¼ pound) shredded cabbage
	Lime wedges

In a large skillet sauté in the butter or margarine the onion, jalapeños, tomatoes, garlic purée, and pepper until heated through. Add the shrimp and lemon and lime juices and cook 5 minutes. Place about 2 tablespoons of filling into each tortilla taco shell. Garnish with the shredded cabbage and lime wedges.

[Variation: You may substitute lobster or white fish pieces for the shrimp.]

MAKES 12 TACOS

Day of the Dead

Skeletons populate El Charro. Larger-than-life papier mâché skeletons stand around wearing charro hats and playing guitars; images of human skeletons hang on the walls. These festive bone men are a salute to the Mexican festival known as the Day of the Dead, a holiday celebrated the first two days of November.

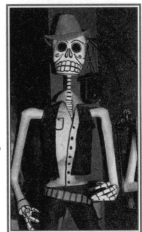

The celebration goes all the way back to Aztec times, and although death is its theme, it is anything but grim or gloomy. The holiday *Dios de los Muertes* acknowledges the natural cycle of death as part of life and pays tribute to the dead with feasts, gifts, and gaiety. Picnics are held at gravesites that have been spruced up with wildly colorful marigolds and religious tokens. In cemeteries throughout Mexico, food, cigarettes, and liquor are left on graves for the dead to enjoy. Shrines are constructed in homes to honor the dear departed and feasts are served while stories about the dead are told and retold.

In this spirit, El Charro's Day of the Dead festivities include the creation of a shrine to founder Monica Flin. Laid out around her photograph are some of her favorite cooking tools, a rosary, bright flowers, and traditional Day of the Dead food items, including sugar skulls, cookies in the shape of skeletons, and special chocolates.

Among the other culinary traditions for this event is the serving of spicy meat dishes and sweet confections galore, plus a special Bread of the Dead (*pan de muerto*) that contains a tiny toy skeleton baked into it. Whoever gets the skeleton is assured good luck for the year to come.

Las Charras Enchiladas de Pollo
Rolled Enchiladas with Chicken

Chicken enchiladas are one of our most popular dishes. We serve them for brunch, lunch, or dinner.

1	quart water
4	large chicken breasts
2	cups oil
12	corn tortillas
2	quarts Enchilada Sauce (page 90)
4	cups (1 pound) longhorn or Jack cheese, shredded

GARNISH:

1	avocado, pitted, peeled, and sliced
2	cups sour cream (optional)

In an 8-quart stockpot bring the water to a boil. Add the chicken breasts, bring to the boil again, reduce heat and simmer 20 minutes, or until the chicken is tender. Drain and cool. Discard the skin and bones. Shred the meat and set aside, covered with a damp towel. Preheat the oven to 350°F (175°C). In a large skillet heat the oil. Dip each tortilla in the oil and place on waxed paper. Place 2 tablespoons chicken in the center of each tortilla and roll each loosely. Place seam side down and side by side in a shallow baking dish. Cover with Salsa de Chile Colorado and a blanket of shredded cheese. Bake in the oven until bubbly, about 10 minutes. Garnish with the avocado slices and sour cream, if using.

MAKES 12 ENCHILADAS

Pechuga de Pollo en Pipián Rápido
Speedy Chicken in Peanut Sauce

As anyone who loves molé can testify, the combination of nuts, garlic, and chile is magical. The peanut sauce that adorns this chicken comes from an ancient recipe that Carlotta says is very complicated. This one is as easy as can be; and the results are dazzling. Serve it with El Charro rice and refried beans.

4	boneless, skinless chicken breasts
1½	cups peanut butter
1	tablespoon garlic purée (page 93)
1	(24-ounce) can red enchilada sauce
1	cup canned chicken broth

Preheat the oven to 350°F (175°C). Spread the chicken breasts with peanut butter and place in a baking dish. Combine the garlic purée with the enchilada sauce and chicken broth. Pour the sauce over the chicken breasts. Bake in the oven 25 minutes, basting the chicken frequently. Remove the chicken to a serving platter. Over high heat, reduce the sauce in the pan and pour over the servings. Serve with El Charro Rice (page 55) and Refried Beans (page 67).

MAKES 4 SERVINGS

Pollo Próspero Año
New Year's Wish Chicken

In many Latin American countries, people insure good luck in the coming year by eating 12 grapes at midnight on New Year's Eve. El Charro's fried chicken recipe calls for thirteen grapes with each serving – one for each month, and one more for extra-good luck.

½	cup sifted flour or Wondra
1	tablespoon garlic powder
1	tablespoon crushed oregano
8	boneless skinless chicken breasts (approximately 6 ounces each)
1	cup of chicken broth
1	cup sliced rings of white onion
½	cup of margarine
¼	cup lemon juice-real lemon
½	cup chopped mango (jar or can is fine—save juice)
½	cup golden raisins
2	cups of pineapple juice (and the remainder of Mango juice from above can/jar)
1	cup of apricot preserves
1	cup or 8 pieces of dried apricot
13	grapes for each chicken breast! (one for each month and one extra for good luck)

Blend flour, garlic, and oregano together and coat the chicken pieces with this mixture. Heat a large non-stick skillet prepared with oil and add the chicken. Pan cook the chicken until it is done through and remove it to a platter and keep warm. In a separate pan, sauté the onion rings in the margarine. Add the lemon juice and simmer slowly. Stir in the chopped mango, raisins, and pineapple/mango juices. Heat the apricot preserves in a microwave and add them to the other sauce ingredients. Continue to simmer. Add the dried apricots and let set a few minutes, then toss in the grapes. Add the cooked chicken and simmer for about 5 minutes until flavors are melded together.

[Notita: Chicken broth can be used to stretch this sauce. Or, if making it one day and not serving it until later, the broth helps to keep the sauce the proper consistency.]

MAKES 8 SERVINGS

Pechugas con Chorizo del Aniversario
80th Anniversary Special Chicken

The year 2002 marks the eightieth anniversary of the restaurant Monica Flin opened in her hometown of Tucson. To celebrate the decades that her great-aunt's creation has endured and thrived, Carlotta created a brilliant recipe that balances the velvety comfort of baked chicken with the punch of *chorizo* (sausage).

8	(6-ounce) boneless chicken breasts		Melted margarine mixed with cilantro (or parsley)
1	pound of soda crackers	½	pound crumbled Mexican cotija cheese (or Greek feta, if the cotija is not available)
1	cup hot water		
½	plus ½ cup condensed milk		
½	pound margarine or butter		**Spicy Tomato Sauce**
1	cup of chopped celery	4	cups whole plum tomatoes
½	cup of chopped white onion	2	cups freshly crushed tomatoes
¼	cup of chopped cilantro (or parsley)	2	tablespoons garlic purée (page 93)
1	tablespoon of garlic purée	1	tablespoon oregano, crushed
½	cup rinsed/chopped green chile	1	cup crumbled Mexican cotija cheese (may substitute feta)
1	pound chorizo (sausage), reserving ½ pound of cooked chorizo for tomato sauce)	½	cup chopped white onion, sautéed in olive oil
8	pieces of dry toast (your choice of bread) with crust removed Garlic salt	1	pint cherry tomatoes, sautéed in olive oil
		1	small can or jar of artichoke quarters (not marinated)

Wash and pat dry chicken breasts and set aside on flat service table. Crush the soda crackers and place them in a bowl with the hot water and ½ cup condensed milk. Set this aside until the crackers have absorbed the liquid. After 1 hour stir the crackers to insure they are all moist. Add the remaining ½ cup condensed milk and mix. Let this stuffing set for 30 minutes. In a large skillet melt the margarine, and then add the celery, onion, cilantro, and garlic. Sauté until the onion is translucent, and then add the cracker mixture by the spoonful, mixing well with the sautéed vegetables. Lightly brown the cracker/vegetable mixture, and then add the chopped green chile and set aside.

In a separate skillet that has been sprayed with nonstick spray, on high heat brown the chorizo. When browned, place the cooked *chorizo* on a paper towel to strain excess grease. Next mix half the *chorizo* with the cracker. (You can save this mixture for the next day.) Save the other half of the *chorizo* for the tomato sauce recipe that follows. Stuff a 1-ounce sized portion of the *chorizo* mix into each breast cavity of the uncooked chicken. Place each stuffed chicken breast on top of single piece of dry toast (crust removed). Place each piece of chicken and toast on a prepared pan. Top each breast with a shake of garlic salt and a drizzle of melted cilantro margarine. On medium heat sautée the chicken breasts until golden brown with an internal temperature of at least 165°F. Remove the chicken breasts from the pan with a spatula and place them on a serving plate and top with the tomato sauce recipe. Finish by sprinkling crumbled Mexican cotija cheese or feta on the top.

To make the Spicy Tomato Sauce, add the remaining cooked, crumbled *chorizo* from the stuffed chicken recipe, and simmer until the sauce begins to boil. This sauce tends to become thicker as it cooks. Don't let it overcook. Break the tomatoes to give body to the sauce, and don't cook until too thick. Add water as needed. Next, serve the chicken breast with a drizzle of the above tomato sauce over the chicken breast. Finish with sprinkle of the above cheese, and add a garnish of green chile strip (you may add other peppers if desired).

MAKES 8 SERVINGS

Pollo Borracho
Grilled Chicken in Spirits

*B*orracho literally means drunk, and it is used by Mexican cooks to describe meat that is marinated in beer or wine. Beer has a way of not only tenderizing chicken, but somehow amplifying its flavor. (Do not marinate for longer than four hours, or the marinade will begin to break up the meat.) As for Carlotta, she makes no secret of the fact that chicken is her favorite meat. It's versatile, low-fat, quick and easy to prepare, and it is adaptable to so many different flavors.

6	*boneless, skinless chicken breasts (1½ to 2 pounds)*

MARINADE:

¼	*cup lime juice*
¼	*cup oil*
12	*ounces dark-brewed Mexican or other beer*
2	*tablespoons garlic purée (page 93)*
2	*cloves, crushed*
1	*cardamom seed, crushed*
1	*bay leaf*
6	*black peppercorns, crushed*
½	*teaspoon salt*

Rinse and pat dry the chicken breasts, trimming the fat. Combine the lime juice, oil, beer, garlic purée, cloves, cardamom, bay leaf, peppercorns, and salt in a large bowl. Add the chicken breasts, turning to coat well. Cover, refrigerate, and marinate at least 3 hours.

Remove the chicken from the marinade, and pat dry. Grill the chicken over charcoal 2 to 5 minutes per side (depending upon thickness of chicken) until cooked through, brushing with the marinade frequently. Slice the chicken and serve as desired, either shredded as filling for tacos, enchiladas, or burros or thinly sliced with cheese between two tortillas for a quesadilla.

MAKES 6 SERVINGS

Tortilla Crusted Chicken

Don't overdo the tortilla-chopping in the blender. While you want them fine and crumbly enough to cling to the chicken, a little textural variety gives the seasoned crust its character.

8	(6-ounce) skinless, boneless chicken breasts
1	cup low-fat milk or low-fat evaporated milk
1	cup flour
3	cups finely crushed tortilla chips (Note: if using a southwestern seasoned chip, the seasoning mix below is not necessary.)

SEASONING MIX:

¼	cup salt
2	tablespoons pepper
2	tablespoons garlic powder
2	tablespoons red cayenne pepper
1	tablespoon dried parsley flakes
	Margarine

Wash and pat dry chicken pieces. Mix the milks in a bowl and drop the chicken pieces into the milk mix. Place the seasoning mix in a plastic bag. Mix the flour and tortilla chips together and place in plastic bag with seasoning mix, remove one piece of chicken at a time and place in bag. Close and shake until fully coated with seasoning mix. Preheat oven to 350°F (175°C). Remove each piece of chicken and place on prepared baking sheet. Carlotta suggests using a butter pan spray on the baking sheet. Place a small dab of margarine on each breast piece for color and moisture. Bake for approximately 45 minutes or until thermometer reaches an internal temperature of 160°F. Serve with your favorite Spanish rice recipe or cheesy potatoes.

MAKES 8 SERVINGS

Pollo y Fideo
Chicken and Pasta

When we were little, our favorite television show was *I Love Lucy*," Carlotta recalls. "My mom would make *Pollo y Fideo* so we could eat from TV trays."

CHICKEN:

3	or 4 whole chicken breasts
½	cup flour
	Salt and pepper
	Vegetable oil
1	(16-ounce) can whole tomatoes
1	(16-ounce) can tomato sauce

SAUCE:

1	pound fideo (vermicelli), cooked al dente
1	onion, sliced
½	pound mushrooms, thickly sliced
1	green or red bell pepper, seeded and sliced
2	to 3 cups crumbled Mexican cheese (casero)
6	to 8 ounces green olives, chopped

Rinse and pat dry the chicken. Cut into serving pieces. Roll in the flour seasoned with salt and pepper to taste. Shake off the excess flour. Heat a large skillet over medium heat. Coat with vegetable oil. Add the chicken carefully and brown. Add the tomatoes and tomato sauce. Bring the mixture up to a simmer, cover, and cook over low heat 15 minutes, less if the chicken pieces are small.

Meanwhile cook the *fideo* in boiling water until al dente. In another skillet, coated lightly with oil, sauté the onion until heated through. Add the mushrooms and bell pepper and sauté briefly. Add this mixture to the chicken, stirring until combined. Cover and cook over low heat 20 to 30 minutes longer, or until the chicken is thoroughly cooked. Serve over the cooked fideo. Sprinkle the crumbled cheese generously over the chicken and garnish with the chopped olives.

[Notita: The last cooking can be done in a 350°F (175°C) oven if that is more convenient. In that case, you may want to assemble the chicken and vegetables in a serving casserole.]

MAKES 6 TO 8 SERVINGS

Pollo Limón y Olivas Verdes
Lemon Chicken with Green Olives

This recipe is a favorite for our summer caterings. It makes a wonderful dish when accompanied by rice and a Caesar salad.

2½	pounds skinned chicken, cut into small pieces
2	tablespoons flour
1	tablespoon olive oil
1	medium onion, chopped
¼	cup chopped garlic, or garlic purée (page 93)
1	cup plus 1½ cups water
⅛	teaspoon saffron
½	teaspoon ground ginger
½	teaspoon ground cumin
½	teaspoon paprika
¼	teaspoon salt
	Grated peel of 2 lemons
3	tablespoons lemon juice
½	cup green olives (pitted and minced)
2	tablespoons finely minced fresh cilantro
	Fresh black pepper

Dust the chicken in the flour. In a large skillet heat the oil over medium heat. Sauté the chicken and the onion-garlic mixture until it has softened. Stir in the 1 cup water and the saffron, ginger, cumin, paprika, salt, and lemon peel. Bring to a boil, and then reduce the heat and simmer, covered, for 35 minutes, adding the remaining 1½ cups water as needed to keep a broth. Add the lemon juice, olives, cilantro, and pepper. Simmer gently for 5 minutes. When done, spoon the chicken and sauce over rice.

MAKES 6 SERVINGS

Pollo en Pipián
Chicken with Pumpkin Seeds and Red Chile Sauce

You will find *Pipián* sauce available ready-made in southwestern markets, but the advantage of making it yourself is that you can amplify its nuttiness by decreasing or even eliminating the pumpkin-seed paste in favor of peanut butter (smooth or chunky).

CHICKEN:		1	*slice bread, toasted and cubed*
6	*chicken breasts (or 3 whole*	¼	*cup garlic purée (page 93)*
breasts split)		3	*cups strained, reserved chicken*
1	*quart water*		*broth (below)*
Pipián Sauce:		⅓	*cup sherry*
4	*dried red chiles*	2	*teaspoons heated oil*
1	*quart water*		*(microwave oil in small glass*
½	*cup dry pumpkin seeds, shelled*		*dish for a few seconds)*
½	*cup blanched almonds*		*Salt*

To prepare the chicken, poach the chicken breasts in the water until cooked through, about 20 minutes. Remove the chicken, and set aside to cool enough to handle. Reserve the chicken broth. Carefully remove and discard the skin and bones from the chicken, leaving the breasts whole.

To make the *Pipián* Sauce, discard the stems from the red chiles; wash and soak the chiles in the water for 15 minutes. Drain. In a dry skillet toast together the pumpkin seeds and almonds, shaking the pan continuously until the seeds and nuts are lightly browned. Do not burn.

Place the toasted seeds and nuts in a blender with the soaked and drained chiles, toasted bread, and garlic purée. Blend to a paste. It will be slightly gritty. Scrape into a large skillet; add the reserved chicken broth and sherry, and simmer over low heat until the sauce thickens. Remove from the heat and whisk in the very hot oil, drop by drop. Return the skillet to the heat and cook slowly, stirring constantly until the fat comes to the surface. Salt to taste.

To assemble, place the cooked chicken into the skillet with the sauce and cook over very low heat about 15 minutes, checking often to make sure the sauce is not scorching.

MAKES 6 SERVINGS

Tacos de Pollo
Chicken Tacos

The traditional way to make a taco, as described in this recipe, is to first dip it quickly in hot oil and then to fry it. However, if you warm a corn tortilla in the microwave oven a few seconds, it will become pliable enough to roll, thus eliminating the need to dip it in hot oil before shaping it. Carlotta also likes to point out that frying is not the only way to cook it. It is also possible to bake tacos.

12	corn tortillas	4	cups shredded lettuce (variety)
2	cups oil, warmed	1	cup canned peas
2	cups poached, shredded chicken breast meat	½	cup sliced radishes
	Salt and pepper	4	cups (1 pound) white, crumbly, Mexican-style cheese or long horn cheese, shredded, or other cheese
GARNISH:			
1	cup shredded green cabbage or lettuce	2	cups Taco Sauce (page 88)

Dip each tortilla in the warm oil and place them on a cookie sheet. Place about 2 tablespoons of the seasoned, shredded chicken at one end of a tortilla. Roll the tortilla around the filling, and secure with a wooden pick. Repeat with the remaining tortillas.

[Notita: It is important to keep tortillas from drying out when working with them by covering them with a damp towel.]

Heat the remaining oil to deep-frying temperature and then place the tacos, two at a time, in the oil, turning them until they are brown on all sides. Drain on paper towels. Remove the picks and serve on a platter. Garnish with the cabbage, lettuce, peas, radishes, cheese, and Taco Sauce.

[Variation: To bake the tacos rather than fry them, place the tacos on a tray in a preheated, 350°F (175°C) oven. Turn two or three times to brown tacos evenly.]

MAKES 12 CHICKEN TACOS

Tacos de Carne
Beef Tacos

Ray Flores Sr. considers beef tacos one of Tucson's defining foods. "Tacos are what made this restaurant famous," he says. In those days, tacos were not necessarily in a hard shell. They were fried, but not to crispness."

Carlotta points out that canned peas are a definite part of the El Charro recipe for tacos. "There is no excuse for them," she teases. "But that's what Monica used, so that's what I use." Radishes are also a Monica legacy; and Carlotta also points to the egg as an uncommon ingredient in most taco recipes. Its purpose is to bind the ingredients into a mini meat loaf.

2	cups oil for deep frying		**GARNISH:**	
½	cup flour	1	cup shredded green cabbage
½	teaspoon salt, or to taste	4	cups shredded lettuce
½	teaspoon ground black pepper	2	cups Taco Sauce (page 88)
¼	cup garlic purée (page 93)	½	cup sliced radishes
1	egg	½	cup canned peas, drained
1	pound lean ground beef	½	pound shredded longhorn
12	corn tortillas		cheese, or other cheese

Heat the oil in a deep fryer or saucepan to 375°F (190°C). Work the flour, salt, pepper, garlic purée, and egg into the beef. Warm the tortillas if they are not pliable. Spread 2 tablespoons of the beef mixture on half of a tortilla. Fold over, press lightly and secure with a wooden pick. Repeat with the remaining tortillas. Fry in the hot oil until crisp. Drain on paper towels. Remove the picks and open the tacos while they are still hot; quickly stuff with the shredded cabbage and lettuce and a tablespoon of taco sauce. Garnish with the radishes and peas and sprinkle generously with the cheese.

[Low-fat notita: By using ground turkey and egg substitute you can lower the fat content considerably.]

[Notita: Shredded, pulled beef, like Machaca (page 143), also works well in tacos. Because the meat is precooked, these tacos can be baked instead of fried.]

MAKES 12 TACOS

World War II Hamburgers

We were the restaurant across from the bus station," Carlotta recalls of El Charro's earlier days. During World War II and in the years that followed, the location attracted a lot of servicemen and women who were coming or going and who stopped at El Charro for a real Tucson meal.

One of the most popular items in those days was Monica's hamburger. Carlotta says that it was made from the same meat set aside to make tacos, but to keep it moist and tender as it grilled, the meat was mixed with bits of wet flour tortilla. Also into the hand-formed patty went chopped white onion. The result was an orb of beef that was high-flavored and juicy.

The menu included fried chicken that had been marinated in spicy *topopo* dressing, along with a salad that included marinated beets and purple onions. There were sliced chicken sandwiches on white bread with Monica's homemade mayonnaise. Monica also put such hot-lunch specials on her menu as leg of lamb made with mint sauce (in which Carlotta reveals the secret ingredient was 7-Up!), roast beef served pot-roast style, even spaghetti and meatballs. T-bone steak dinners were always a popular item, as were steak sandwiches served with sliced apples and melted cheese.

Carlotta also notes that in those days, El Charro was like so many Southwestern restaurants in that it served *menudo* every weekend evening. The old-time tripe and hominy stew, said to prevent, or at least to cure, hangovers, was always a popular item late at night and just before Monica finally shut her doors at two in the morning on Friday and Saturday nights. "We have never given in to the 2 A.M. closing time," Carlotta, says. "Consequently, we do not serve *menudo*."

Barbacoa
Barbecued Beef

*B*arbacoa is rich, fragrant shredded beef that is wonderful heaped on a plate accompanied by grilled corn on the cob or served in any tortilla-pocketed dish. ·

MEAT:

2   quarts water

3   pounds roast beef (eye of round
       or brisket), cut into 12 pieces

¼   cup garlic purée (page 93)

1¼   ounces pickling spice*, tied in
       cheesecloth pouch

1   teaspoon salt

BARBECUE SAUCE:

4   tablespoons oil

½   cup chopped fresh Anaheim
       chiles, roasted (page 79)

1   white onion, chopped

¼   cup garlic purée (page 93)

1   tablespoon vinegar

1   cup reserved meat broth

1   (8-ounce) can jalapeños,
       drained, thinly sliced

1   tablespoon juice from canned
       jalapeños

1   bay leaf

½   cup Enchilada Sauce (page 90)

1   teaspoon ground black pepper

½   cup green olives, minced

4   large tomatoes, chopped

½   cup wine

Bring the water to a boil and add the beef, garlic purée, spice pouch, and salt. Bring to a boil again, skim the froth, reduce the heat, and simmer for 1 hour, or until the meat is tender, removing the froth as it accumulates. Remove the meat and let it cool enough to handle. Discard the spice pouch; reserve the liquid. Shred the meat by pulling apart the fibers with your fingers. Preheat the oven to 300°F (150°C). In a large skillet heat the oil and sauté the green chiles, onion, garlic purée, vinegar, broth, jalapeños, and jalapeño juice. Add the bay leaf. Add the shredded meat and the salsa, black pepper, green olives, tomatoes, and wine. Simmer for about 10 minutes. Remove and discard the bay leaf. Place the seasoned meat in a large, shallow baking pan, and bake for about 1 hour, stirring occasionally.

MAKES 6 TO 8 SERVINGS

*Combine in the cheesecloth pouch cloves, cinnamon-stick pieces, whole coriander seed, bay leaf, peppercorns, and other whole spices or herbs that appeal to you.

Carne Asada
Grilled Skirt Steak

Carne asada is grilled meat—usually in a charbroiler—and this is a truly simple and delicious way of cooking. In this case, I use tender marinated skirt steaks, thinly sliced and rolled into a tortilla with fresh salsa and guacamole.

4	pounds skirt steak (Flank steaks will work, but they need more marinating time.)
½	cup cider vinegar
½	cup vegetable oil
1	tablespoon coarse ground pepper
1	tablespoon crushed red pepper
1	teaspoon dried oregano

Rinse and pat dry the steaks and place them in a glass baking dish. Combine the vinegar, oil, peppers, and oregano and pour the marinade over the top of the meat. Turn the steaks to coat both sides of the meat. Cover and refrigerate at least 5 hours, turning the meat occasionally. Prepare the grill. When the coals are medium hot, place the meat on the grill, and cook for about 5 to 6 minutes on each side. Slice across the grain, and serve with fresh salsa, guacamole, and flour tortillas. A garnish of fresh lime or orange segments will add a zest to your grilled meat.

MAKES 6 TO 8 SERVINGS

Carne Verde
Green Chile and Beef Stew

Carlotta refers to carne verde as "just beef-and-potato stew," reminiscent of ancestors on her Irish father's side. The potatoes, as well as the tomatoes, are anathema in a Texas bowl of red; but in the cultural melting pot that is Tucson, the combination of ingredients makes perfect sense.

3	quarts water	½	cup oil
3	pounds roast beef (eye of round, brisket, or chuck), cut into 12 pieces	¼	cup garlic purée (page 93)
		2	tablespoons flour
		1	cup reserved broth
1	tablespoon salt	8	fresh Anaheim chiles, roasted
1	tablespoon ground black pepper	2	large potatoes, cooked, peeled, and cubed
1	plus 1 medium white onion, 1 quartered; 1 sliced		
		2	large tomatoes, cubed

In an 8-quart stockpot bring the water to a boil. Add the meat, salt, pepper, and the quartered onion and simmer for 2 hours, or until the meat is tender. Remove the froth frequently. Remove the meat, and let it cool. Reserve the broth and cut the cooled meat into ½-inch pieces, removing the fat.

In a large skillet heat the oil and sauté the sliced onion until soft but not brown. Stir in the meat, a little at a time. Add the garlic purée, stir, and simmer on low. Meanwhile, dissolve the flour in a small amount of reserved broth; then combine the flour with the remaining cup of broth and add to the meat. Gently fold in the chiles, potatoes, and tomatoes and simmer until bubbling. Taste and adjust the seasonings.

[Notita: This is a basic meat preparation that we serve in bowls with tortillas, on combination plates, or as filling for burros, chimis, and chalupas. To stretch the meat—or cut down on the amount of meat you eat—serve the stew over rice or noodles.]

MAKES 6 TO 8 SERVINGS

Chile Colorado/Chile con Carne
Red Chile and Beef Stew

"The dish by which you can judge the quality of a Mexican restaurant," according to Carlotta, Chile Colorado is little more than beef and red chiles with a little spice. Its customary presentation is in a bowl; but if cooked thick enough, it makes ideal filling for burros and chimichangas.

3	pounds roast beef (eye of round, chuck, brisket, or half a boneless pork roast)
1	cup flour
1	tablespoon salt
1	teaspoon ground black pepper
½	cup oil
3	cups Enchilada Sauce (page 90)
1	tablespoon garlic purée (page 93)
1	teaspoon dried oregano

Cut the meat into ¾-inch pieces, and place, a handful at a time, into a paper bag containing the flour, salt, and pepper. Shake well. Repeat with the remaining meat. In a large skillet heat the oil. Add the meat, a batch at a time so the skillet is not crowded, and brown slowly. Add the Salsa de Chile Colorado, garlic purée, and oregano. Cook over low heat 1 hour or longer, or until meat is tender, stirring frequently to prevent scorching. Add a little hot water if necessary.

MAKES 6 TO 8 SERVINGS

Carne Seca

Dried beef is common to many cuisines, especially in the South-west, but no one makes *carne seca* like El Charro. The exact recipe for the meat's marinade is a closely held family secret, but it is no mystery how it is dried. Monica Flin used to hang strips of beef on a clothesline in a storage shed. Today the Flores family takes advantage of the desert sun and hoists strips of marinated thin-sliced tenderloin up above the patio off El Charro's south-facing roof. The beef is held in a metal mesh cage that keeps it safe from flying critters, but leaves it in the open air to dry for several hours. Suspended on ropes and pulleys, the cage sways above the patio, wafting a faint perfume of lemon and garlic into the Arizona air. The infusion of the marinade and the caress of a clean desert breeze transform this beef from something merely meaty into an eating experience that is wild and profound. This is meat that has blossomed—glistening mahogany and fairly dripping flavor, dry and yet somehow deliriously succulent, rugged but a pure pleasure to chew. After it is air-dried, *carne seca* is shredded, spiced, sautéed, and generally served in concert with sweet onions, hot chiles, and tomatoes, often inside burros and tacos.

Machaca
Carne Seca Substitute

The most essential ingredient for true carne seca, El Charro style, is available only in and around Tucson: southwestern sun. The recipe shared by the Flores family for dried beef is therefore something other than their kitchen's own carne seca . . . but it does a good imitation as the essential ingredient in tacos (fried or baked) or spread across tostados grandes.

3	*quarts water*
¼	*plus ¼ plus ¼ cup garlic purée (page 93)*
4	*to 6 pounds roast beef, shredded*
	Juice of 2 limes
⅓	*cup oil*
1	*cup chopped fresh Anaheim chiles, roasted (page 79)*
½	*teaspoon salt*
½	*teaspoon ground black pepper*
½	*white onion, sliced into rings*
2	*tomatoes, chopped*
	Shredded roast beef

To cook the meat, in an 8-quart stockpot bring the water to a boil. Add ¼ cup garlic purée and the meat and return to a boil. Skim off the froth, reduce the heat, and simmer for about 2 hours, or until the meat is tender. Remove the froth as needed. Drain and reserve the juices.

To brown and dry the meat, combine the lime juice and ¼ cup garlic purée. Preheat the oven to 325°F (165°C). Spread the shredded meat in a single layer on a large cookie sheet and sprinkle with the lime juice mixed with garlic purée. Roast the meat until brown and as dry as you choose, at least 15 minutes, and up to an hour, stirring occasionally.

[Notita: At this point you may cool, cover, and refrigerate or freeze the meat for later use.]

To fry the meat, heat the oil in a large skillet. Sauté the chile peppers with the salt and pepper. Add the onion and tomatoes and sauté briefly; then add the remaining ¼ cup garlic purée. Add the meat, stirring over medium heat to brown. If too dry, add some reserved juices.

MAKES 12 SERVINGS

Empanadas de Carne
Beef Turnovers

While the following meat filling is traditional in empanadas, consider also using *Picadillo* to fill the wieldy turnovers. Always serve empanadas warm, either fresh from the oven or, if necessary, reheated.

FILLING:		**PASTRY:**	
2	pounds lean ground beef	3	cups flour
½	cup raisins	1	teaspoon baking powder
1	teaspoon ground cinnamon	3	tablespoons chilled shortening
¼	cup sugar	1	egg, beaten
1	teaspoon salt	1	cup ice water
1	teaspoon garlic purée (page 93)		
½	teaspoon chopped pinon nuts or pecans		

Preheat the oven to 400°F (205°C). Brown the meat in a large skillet over medium heat, stirring and breaking apart the meat so that it browns evenly. Add the raisins, cinnamon, sugar, salt, garlic purée, and nuts, mixing well over medium heat. If too dry, add a few tablespoons of water. Set aside to cool while preparing the pastry.

[Notita: This basic, rich pastry can be made ahead, refrigerated or frozen. If you want a less-rich pastry, omit the egg and adjust the liquid.]

To make the pastry, combine the flour and baking powder in a large bowl. Cut in the shortening with a pastry blender or two knives until dough is the consistency of coarse meal. Add the beaten egg, mixing just until blended. Slowly add enough chilled water, mixing now with your hands, until the dough forms into a ball. (Over mixing or allowing your hands to heat up the dough will make the dough tough. If necessary, chill the dough before handling further.)

On a well-floured surface, roll out the dough to ¼ to ½ inch thick. Cut out circles with a biscuit cutter or the rim of a drinking glass. Fill each circle with 1 tablespoonful of the meat mixture. Fold the circle in half, making a half circle, and crimp the edges to seal in the filling. Place the filled empanadas on an ungreased cookie sheet and bake in the oven for 15 to 20 minutes, or until browned. Serve immediately or rewarm later.

MAKES 28 TO 30 EMPANADAS

Picadillo

Hash

You won't attend a Mexican wedding without sampling *Picadillo*. No one can explain for sure why this hash of meat and potatoes with sweet and savory spices has become such a tradition for nuptial meals, but Carlotta surmises that it is appropriate for a young couple because "it makes everyone feel at home and is not costly to prepare."

½	teaspoon salt
¼	cup water
2	pounds lean chopped or ground beef
¼	cup garlic purée (page 93)
½	white onion, chopped
2½	cups diced, cooked potato
2	celery ribs, chopped
1	medium tomato, peeled and diced
¼	cup raisins, soaked in hot water until plump
8	tablespoons vinegar
½	cup ketchup mixed with ½ cup water (optional)
6	green olives, pitted and chopped
1	to 2 teaspoons sugar (optional)
	Cinnamon
1	cup diced, unpeeled apple

Heat a skillet and add the salt, water, and ground beef. Stir and separate the beef, and brown it quickly. Add the garlic purée, onion, potato, celery, tomato, raisins, vinegar, ketchup, olives, sugar, cinnamon, and apples. Cook until flavors blend, about 15 minutes, stirring frequently.

[Notita: Use Spanish green olives in this recipe. Ketchup sweetens Picadillo; so, if the apples are tart, you might choose to add a little.]

MAKES 6 TO 8 SERVINGS

Chuletas de Puerco con Olivas y Naranjas
Pork Chops with Olives and Oranges

This special-occasion dish calls for the very best trimmed, thick, center-cut pork chops.

6	center-cut pork chops
2	tablespoons oil
1	onion, chopped
1	cup beef or chicken broth
1	cup orange juice
½	teaspoon dried oregano
2	tablespoons garlic purée (page 93)
	Salt and pepper
1	(6-ounce) jar pimiento-stuffed Spanish olives, drained
1	tablespoon cornstarch
2	tablespoons cold water
2	cups orange sections

Rinse and pat dry the pork chops. Trim the excess fat. Heat the oil in a large skillet and brown the chops evenly over medium heat. Remove the chops, and set aside. In the same skillet brown the onion. Carefully add the broth, orange juice, oregano, garlic purée, and salt and pepper to taste. Return the chops to the skillet; sprinkle the olives over all. Cover, reduce heat to simmer, and cook about 45 minutes until tender. Mix together the cold water and cornstarch. Add to the liquid in the skillet, and stir to blend. Let thicken, and then add the orange sections before serving.

[Notita: A temperature that is too high tends to toughen pork chops, if too low, they dry out.]

MAKES 6 SERVINGS

Carnitas de Puerco
Shredded Pork

When large pieces of pork are on sale, prepare a big batch of carnitas and freeze some," Carlotta suggests. Like shredded beef, this pork is handy on a combination plate and is the right texture for filling either corn or flour tortillas.

2	*pounds pork loin*
1	*onion, cut in half*
2	*carrots, cut into 1-inch pieces*
1	*whole head garlic, separated, peeled if desired*
1	*teaspoon salt*

Rinse and pat dry the pork loin. Place the pork loin, onion, carrots, garlic, and salt in a large kettle with water to cover. Bring to a boil; reduce the heat and simmer about 1 hour. Remove meat to cool; reserve liquid.

When the pork is cool enough to handle, shred it by pulling apart the fibers with your fingers. Carnitas freeze beautifully if you add some of the reserved cooking liquid to the freezer container to fill it completely.

MAKES 4 TO 6 SERVINGS

Chorizo
Mexican Sausage

Mexican sausage is rarely sold as tubular links. Butchers sell it loose, like chopped beef, by the pound; and Mexican cooks make it not only for lunch and supper, but for breakfast, either sautéed with potatoes and served with eggs and tortillas or as the filling of a breakfast burro. Sunday brunches at El Charro always include a scramble of *chorizo* and eggs, accompanied by refried beans, fried potatoes, and warm tortillas.

6	*pounds lean ground beef (or half ground pork or ground turkey)*
2	*cups white wine*
1	*cup wine vinegar*
3	*teaspoons salt*
4	*tablespoons dried oregano*
½	*cup garlic purée (page 93)*
8	*ounces ground red chile powder*
2	*quarts Salsa Adobo (page 84)*

Combine the ground meat, wine, and vinegar thoroughly. Add the salt, oregano, and garlic purée. Add the chile powder gradually, kneading it in with your hands. Gradually knead in the chile paste. Place in a large ceramic bowl, cover with plastic, and refrigerate overnight. Drain any liquid. Use in a day or two, or divide into meal-size portions and freeze.

[Notita: Wear vinyl gloves when kneading this mixture; otherwise you'll have orange fingernails for a day or two.]

YIELD: 6 POUNDS

¡Costillas de Puerco Estilo Pibil-Sin Ojas!
Ribs with Mango and Fresh Mint Salsa

Carlotta is a big fan of mangos and loves combining them with other fruits for salsas to accompany almost any kind of chicken or pork. In this case, the distinctive sweet/salty mango flavor is laced with mint for a rib glaze that is heavenly.

Rack of 6 to 8 pork ribs, any cut, boneless or country style

RECADO (MARINADE):

1	(3-ounce) package achiote paste
½	cup orange juice
½	cup warm water
1	tablespoon crushed garlic
½	teaspoon oregano

MANGO AND FRESH MINT SALSA:

2	cups mango pieces (jar, canned, or fresh)
¼	cup diced purple onion
¼	cup fresh, chopped mint leaves
1	teaspoon salt
1	teaspoon red pepper flakes
	Juice of 2 oranges
2	oranges, cut in segments, for garnish

Dissolve the achiote paste (usually found in block form) in a blender with the orange juice, warm water, garlic, and oregano. Set aside. Trim, wash, and pat dry the ribs. Place the recado in a bowl. Bathe the ribs in the marinade, and let them sit for 20 minutes. Rotate the ribs, and let sit 20 more minutes. Preheat the oven to 350°F (175°C). Place the ribs in a baking pan, and bake until done. Transfer the ribs to a serving platter; serve with the mango and fresh mint salsa, and garnish with the orange segments.

While the ribs are baking, mix together the mango pieces, onion, mint leaves, salt, and pepper flakes, and squeeze in the orange juice. Allow the flavors to meld.

MAKES 4 SERVINGS

Costillas de Puerco en Salsa Chipotle
Pork Ribs in Pepper Sauce

Chipotle chiles have a smoky heat that brings out the sweetness of pork ribs in a way that is similar to the effect of Midwestern barbecue sauce. It's a balance of heat-and-sweet that makes tastebuds restless for more, more, more.

5	*pounds pork ribs, cracked and trimmed*
2	*cans chipotle chiles in adobo sauce*
1	*cup Enchilada Sauce (page 90)*
1	*tablespoon salt*
1	*tablespoon black pepper*
1	*large onion, chopped*
	Orange slices

Preheat the oven to 325°F (165°C). Wash and pat dry the pork ribs. Place them on a baking sheet and bake for 25 to 30 minutes. Turn and continue to bake for another 30 minutes, or until the meat pulls away from the bone easily. Remove from the oven and transfer the ribs to a clean baking dish. Add the chipotle chiles to the red chile sauce along with the salt and pepper and spread over the ribs. Add the chopped onion and 3 tablespoons of browned meat juice. Return the ribs to the oven, and bake for 10 more minutes. If you have any sauce left, add it to the ribs during the second baking. Garnish with orange slices, and serve.

MAKES 6 TO 8 SERVINGS

Puerco Adobado
Pork Ribs with Red Chile

Few other ingredients bring out the sweet succulence of pork better than earthy chiles with at least a bit of bite. Marinated in El Charro's Adobo sauce (page 84), spare ribs or baby back ribs develop a lip-tingling intensity that stimulates both appetite and thirst and makes eating them a virtual addiction.

1	cup Salsa Adobo (page 84)
¾	cup vinegar
1	teaspoon salt, or to taste
1	teaspoon dried oregano
3	pounds pork ribs

In a small bowl, combine the red chile paste, vinegar, salt, and oregano to make a marinade. Rub the marinade into the pork ribs, cover, and refrigerate at least 4 hours, turning occasionally. Preheat the oven to 350°F (175°C) and roast the ribs about 1 hour, or until tender.

MAKES 6 SERVINGS

Desserts

(Postres)

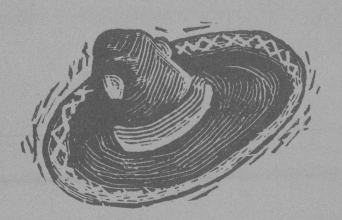

It is common to pay dessert short shrift in Mexican-American restaurants. After all, who has room for pudding after tucking into a plate-sized burrito? In fact, the Mexican dessert repertoire is rich and fascinating, if for no other reason than the curious roles that chocolate plays. Sweets play an especially important role in celebrating the Day of the Dead, when bakers produce special breads and pastries and confectioners make candies in the shape of favorite animals, coffins, and skeletons. El Charro's Day of the Dead menu always features Pumpkin Tamales.

Plátanos de Hacienda
House Bananas

For anyone with an ambitious sweet tooth, these "house bananas" are a must-eat dish. Carlotta suggests serving them with warm coffee or Mexican hot chocolate, either as dessert or as a pick-me-up snack.

3	tablespoons brown sugar
1	tablespoon powdered cinnamon
8	ripe bananas, sliced lengthwise (not in disks)
1	cup of shredded/unsweetened coconut
½	cup of melted butter
½	cup of rum
4	tablespoons pineapple juice
½	cup of pineapple purée
1	quart vanilla ice cream
	Whipped cream
	Cinnamon
½	cup toasted and diced walnuts

Mix the brown sugar and cinnamon together. Preheat the oven to 350°F (175°C). Butter a baking sheet and arrange the bananas with the cut side facing down. Sprinkle the bananas with the sugar/cinnamon mix, drizzle with melted butter, and sprinkle with shredded coconut. Bake 8 to 10 minutes until the coconut starts to turn golden brown. Heat the rum, pineapple juice, and all but a couple of tablespoons of the pineapple purée together until warm. Strain and ladle the juice/rum mix onto serving plates. Arrange the cooked warm bananas on the plates over a generous scoop of vanilla ice cream. Top with the whipped cream, sprinkled with cinnamon and chopped walnuts. For a final touch add a dab of the reserved warm pineapple purée on top.

MAKES 8 SERVINGS

Almendrado
Almond Meringue Pudding

Almendrado is popular throughout the year, but you'll see more of it eaten around Mexican Independence Day, when it is molded in layers of green, white, and red to resemble the flag. Folk wisdom says that if the *Almendrado* fails, it is a signal that the cook is angry.

	Vegetable oil spray
1	*envelope (1 scant tablespoon) unflavored gelatin*
¼	*cup cold water*
6	*egg whites at room temperature*
¾	*cup sugar*
1	*teaspoon almond extract*
	Red and green food coloring
½	*cup slivered almonds*

CUSTARD SAUCE:

6	*egg yolks*
⅓	*cup sugar*
	Pinch of salt
1	*cup milk*
1	*cup cream*
½	*teaspoon vanilla*

GARNISH:

2	*cups whipped cream (sweetened if desired)*
½	*cup slivered almonds*

Lightly grease a loaf pan, or spray with vegetable oil, and chill. Also chill a large bowl to be used to beat the egg whites. In a small saucepan, sprinkle the gelatin over ¼ cup cold water. Let stand 5 minutes to soften; then place over very low heat and stir until dissolved. Set aside to cool. Separate the eggs, making sure none of the yolk contaminates the whites. In the large, chilled bowl, and with oil-free, dry beaters, beat the whites until firm peaks form, gradually beating in ¾ cup sugar. Beat in the almond extract and cooled gelatin in a thin stream. Place one-third of the beaten whites into a bowl, and blend in a few drops of red food coloring. Spread into a loaf pan. Spread half the remaining untinted whites over the pink layer. Add a few drops of green food coloring to the remaining whites, and spread over the white layer. Top with the slivered almonds. Chill 2 hours, or until firm. Cover with plastic wrap after chilling so a gummy skin does not form.

To make the custard sauce, in a 2-quart saucepan, beat the egg yolks. Add the sugar, salt, milk, and cream. Stir constantly over medium heat until the custard thickens, about 20 minutes. Do not boil. Remove from the heat; let cool. Add the vanilla extract to the cooled custard, or it may curdle. Pour into a one-quart pitcher; cover and chill.

[Notita: This sauce can be tricky. If it starts to get too thick while cooking, immediately pour it into a cool saucepan, and plunge it into a pan of cold water. If the sauce is somewhat lumpy after cooking, strain it, and add milk to thin.]

Unmold the *Almendrado*, if desired, and serve in ¾-inch-wide slices. Place a slice on a plate and drizzle the custard sauce in a 2-inch-wide strip across the slice, not hiding the flag.

[Low-fat variation: Use egg substitute and nonfat milk. Omit the whipped cream.]

[Notita: For special occasions, we sometimes add whipped cream and slivered almonds for garnish.]

[Notita: It is best to bring eggs to room temperature before using them so they will separate well. Set aside enough time to complete the dessert. If you start and are interrupted, the egg whites will fall.]

MAKES 12 SERVINGS

Capirotada
Lenten Bread Pudding

One of the strangest, and yet most typical Mexican desserts is this sweet pudding that includes cheese, onions and cilantro, known as "A-Little-Bit-Of-Everything-Good Pudding." Its point is to have all the ingredients necessary to fortify oneself after a long fast.

6	cloves
¼	cup fresh cilantro
¼	cup chopped green onion tops
3	sticks cinnamon
2	cones piloncillo, crushed, or 4 cups dark brown sugar
1	quart water
½	pound margarine, melted
2	loaves French bread, sliced
1	cup dark raisins
2	tablespoons chopped walnuts or pecans
3	cups crumbled Mexican (or Jack) cheese, shredded

GARNISH:

1	pint heavy cream, whipped (sweetened, if desired)

Preheat the oven to 325°F (165°C). Wrap the cloves, cilantro, onion tops, and cinnamon in cheesecloth and boil with the piloncillo in the water for 10 minutes, or until syrupy. Meanwhile, spread the margarine on the bread slices and toast both sides lightly under the broiler. Place half the toast in a 13 x 11-inch glass baking pan. Spread half the raisins, half the nuts, and half the syrup over the toast. Sprinkle with half the cheese. Repeat the layering with remaining ingredients. Cover with foil and bake 30 minutes. Serve warm topped with whipped cream.

[Notita: Chopped apples and additional chopped nuts may be added for extra flavor and nutrition.]

MAKES 8 TO 12 SERVINGS

Arroz con Leche
Rice Pudding

There are no rules for rice pudding," Carlotta declares, meaning you can add whatever other sweet ingredients or nuts you see fit, or you can eliminate the nuts or raisins.

1	cup rice
½	stick cinnamon
⅛	teaspoon salt
1	cup water
1	cup sugar
¾	cup milk, nonfat milk, or cream
¼	cup seedless white or dark raisins
2	egg yolks or equivalent egg substitute
	Grated peel of ½ lemon or orange
¼	cup chopped almonds, pecans, or pine nuts

Combine the rice, cinnamon stick, and salt in the water in a saucepan. Cover and bring to the boil. Reduce the heat immediately and steam until the rice absorbs the water, about 10 minutes. Discard the cinnamon stick. Add the sugar, milk, and raisins to the rice, stirring lightly, not breaking up rice. Cover and let stand so the milk is absorbed by the rice, about 10 minutes. Beat the egg yolks and, stirring constantly, slowly stir the yolks into the rice mixture. Return to low heat and stir in the grated peel. Cook 5 minutes more, being careful not to let the mixture burn. Chill. Serve topped with the nuts.

[Notita: A nonstick saucepan is safest.]

MAKES 4 SERVINGS

Flan
Caramel Custard

Traditional flan is made with vanilla flavoring, but it is possible to substitute other extracts, such as almond or espresso, to give it a unique taste.

½	plus ¼ cup sugar
6	eggs, lightly beaten
	Pinch of salt
1	teaspoon vanilla extract
1	quart scalded milk

GARNISH:

Whipped cream
Dash of Kahlúa liqueur
Slivered almonds

Caramelize the ½ cup sugar by heating it in a skillet over very low heat, stirring constantly while it melts and turns brown. (Don't cook past this point or it will harden into amber glass.) Pour the caramel into individual custard cups, or pour into a 6-cup, shallow baking dish. Combine the beaten eggs, the remaining ¼ cup sugar, salt, and vanilla, beating well with a whisk. Stir in the scalded milk. Strain into the baking dish over the caramel coating. Preheat the oven to 350°F (175°C). Place the baking dish in a roasting pan, and add enough hot water in the roasting pan to come halfway up the sides of the baking dish. Bake for 20 to 30 minutes. Insert a knife into the center of the custard. If it comes out clean, the custard is set. Cool and chill before serving; garnish with whipped cream flavored with the liqueur and almonds.

[Notita: You'll need to make a bain marie (water bath) for this custard. The shallow, 6-cup baking dish you choose should fit inside a roasting pan so the baking dish is surrounded with hot water while baking. If using individual custard cups, place them in one large bain marie (water bath).]

MAKES 8 TO 12 SERVINGS

The Haunted Basement

The building that houses El Charro today was constructed by Jules Flin, Monica's father, as a family home in the late 1890s. The family home was located just outside the old Mexican *Presidio* in a part of town known as Snob Hollow. Flin owned the whole block, which was an exclusive area, but not exactly luxurious by today's standards. Arizona was still disputed territory, and Flin kept his Winchesters loaded and ready for fear of raids by Chiricahua Apaches. (Geronimo had been captured fewer than ten years earlier.) Flin's home was a solid structure, and it featured one of the few basements in Tucson; he even built underground passageways connecting his house to others in the neighborhood. He used the rock-walled basement as a cool place to store homemade cheese and wine. Toward the end of his life, it was in the basement he chose to live.

"He swore and carried on down there when he was old," Carlotta remembers her mother telling her. "And he could be mean. When finally he did pass away, people could not imagine this house without his presence as part of it, and in a sense, he never left. My mother had a great imagination and was a believer in the spirit world. She would tell us that if we did not behave, we would be sent to the basement to face ¡El Diablo! That was Jules Flin's ghost, who has now become part of the El Charro legend. Over the years, we have heard doors slam and bottles crash to the floor mysteriously, but I don't believe that Jules Flin is a menacing ghost. He just wants us to remember that his spirit is here, that our family and the family home he built has been part of Tucson since long ago."

Yazmin's Choco Flan

Flan is baked in a bain marie to become an ineffably tender custard. While "plain" flan has the pure cooked-sugar flavor of caramel, choco-flan electrifies that simple formula with a devilish chocolate shot.

1	cup Cajeta (Mexican candy, Kraft caramels can be substituted)

CAKE:

1⅔	cups all-purpose flour, or 2 cups cake flour
1⅔	cups sugar
⅔	cup cocoa
1½	teaspoons baking soda
1	teaspoon salt
1½	cups buttermilk
½	cup shortening
2	eggs
1	teaspoon vanilla

FLAN:

1	can condensed milk
1	can evaporated milk
3	eggs
2	egg whites
2	teaspoons vanilla

To make the cake, grease a baking pan with the *cajeta* (caramel). Use the whole cup. Beat the flour, sugar, cocoa, baking soda, salt, buttermilk, shortening, eggs, and vanilla in a mixing bowl on low speed, mixing the batter constantly for at least 30 seconds. Beat on high for 3 minutes. Pour the batter into the pan.

To make the flan, beat the condensed milk, evaporated milk, eggs, egg whites, and vanilla in a large mixing bowl on high speed for 2 minutes and then pour the flan mixture into the pan on top of the cake mixture. Let the pan with the flan and the chocolate cake sit out for 20 minutes. Preheat the oven to 350°F (175°C). Bake for 45 minutes.

MAKES 1 CAKE

Azúcar Dulce
Sugar Candy

For those who consider sugar not sugary enough, Azúcar Dulce is the remedy. It is sugar squared, buttered, and enriched . . . and served in bite-sized portions of overwhelming sweetness.

1	cup chopped pecans
1	cup dark brown sugar
1	cup half-and-half
4	tablespoons butter
2	tablespoons corn syrup
2	tablespoons rum extract

Prepare a cookie sheet with butter. Place the pecans, brown sugar, half-and-half, butter, corn syrup, and rum in a ceramic bowl. Place the bowl over a bain marie (water bath or double broiler), and bring to a boil. Cook until a spoonful dropped on the cookie sheet holds its shape. Proceed to drop spoonfuls on the cookie sheet and let cool. Remove and place in candy paper cups, or small pieces of wax paper.

[Notita: Cooking foods in banana leaves is a style of cooking referred to as pibil. *The flavoring that is used to marinate the meat is called* recado *and is made from the annatto seeds, easily found in the ethnic areas of the Mexican food department in your favorite store; they are packaged as* achiote paste.

[Notita: Any marinade can cause the food to lose its integrity if left too long in the marinade. Since the food may dry out or become too salty, too mushy, or too stringy, it is important to monitor it. Marinades are to impart flavor, not be the reason to lose flavor.]

MAKES 2¼ CUPS

Tequila-Based Dessert Syrup

Use this intoxicating syrup as a topping over fresh fruit, pastries, or ice cream as a dessert.

1	cup corn syrup (or Agave nectar found in health food stores)
1	cup lime juice
1	teaspoon cayenne
¼	cup Cuervo Tradicional

In a saucepan place the corn syrup, lime juice, and cayenne and heat until boiling. Add the tequila and ignite it with a match as a *flambé* (be careful not to do so near a draft and avoid skin contact). Shake the pan until the flame extinguishes itself and use this as a topping over fresh fruit, pastries, ice cream, etc. Finish off your sweets with a garnish of fresh mint leaf, fresh coconut, or glazed nuts.

MAKES 2¼ CUPS

Rosca de Reyes
Three Kings Bread

The Day of the Epiphany, January 6, is known as Little Christmas. It is tradition to serve Three Kings Bread with a small charm inside. The person who is served the slice of bread containing the charm is obliged to give a party on Candlemass Day in February. Carlotta reminds us, "If you do add a charm, be sure to warn your guests to look for it!"

1	pound butter or margarine
1	pound powdered sugar
6	eggs
4	cups cake flour
¼	teaspoon baking powder
1	teaspoon vanilla
1	cup chopped walnuts or pecans

SYRUP:

2	cups brown sugar
1	teaspoon ground anise
1	teaspoon vanilla extract

Preheat the oven to 350°F (175°C). In a large mixing bowl cream together the butter or margarine and powdered sugar. Add the eggs and beat again until light and fluffy. Combine the cake flour and baking powder. Gradually add them to the creamed mixture along with the vanilla. Sprinkle the nuts on the bottom of a lightly greased 9 x 5 x 4-inch loaf pan. Pour the batter into the pan on top of the nuts. Bake for 55 minutes, or until a tester pick comes out clean and the cake springs back to the touch. Cool 10 minutes, then turn the cake out onto a wire rack to cool completely.

To make the syrup, melt the brown sugar in a heavy saucepan over low heat. Add the ground anise and vanilla extract. Pour the warm syrup over the freshly baked cake.

MAKES ONE 9 X 5-INCH LOAF

Tamales de Calabaza
Sweet Pumpkin Tamales

If you are looking for something sweet to end the meal around Halloween time, look no further. These pumpkin tamales are a wonderful dessert, especially in the autumn. It is traditional to eat them for breakfast for *Dia de Los Muertos* at the beginning of November, when confectioners also prepare sweets shaped like coffins, lambs, rabbits, and skulls. Carlotta notes that if fresh *masa* is available, use it and eliminate the chicken broth.

MASA:

¾	cup vegetable shortening
1	cup sugar
1	teaspoon salt
2	teaspoons baking powder
3½	cups (1 pound) premixed masa
2½	cups warm chicken broth

FILLING:

1½	cups (16 ounces) canned pumpkin
1	(5-ounce) can evaporated milk
¾	cup sugar
2	teaspoons ground cinnamon
½	teaspoon ground nutmeg
1	teaspoon vanilla extract
½	cup coconut
½	cup crushed pineapple
¼	cup chopped pecans or raisins (optional)
	Dried corn husks
	Pineapple Chutney (recipe follows)

For masa, whip the vegetable shortening until fluffy, about 5 minutes. Beat in the sugar, salt, and baking powder. Add the premixed *masa* and broth alternately, beating until well mixed. Let it stand at room temperature for 5 minutes.

For the filling, in a saucepan combine the pumpkin, milk, sugar, cinnamon, and nutmeg. Over medium heat, bring the mixture to a boil, and cook for one minute. Remove from the heat. Stir in the vanilla extract, coconut, pineapple, and pecans or raisins, if using. Set the mixture aside to cool completely.

To assemble, soak the corn husks in hot water for about 30 minutes, to soften. Remove, and wipe off any extra water. Separate the corn husks. In the center of each husk, spread about 2 tablespoons of the *masa*. Spoon 1 tablespoon of the filling lengthwise down the center of *masa*. Fold the husk over the filling to encase it. (Use two husks if necessary.) Fold the bottom, pointed end up, over the enclosed filling. Place the tamales, open end up, in a steamer basket or Dutch oven fitted with a rack. Do not crowd. If necessary, place extra husks among the tamales to keep them upright. Place a layer of husks over the tamales; cover and steam about 1¼ to 1½ hours. To serve, open the husks, and top with 2 tablespoons of warm pineapple chutney.

MAKES 24 TAMALES

Cajeta de Piña
Pineapple Chutney

This is the garnish for pumpkin tamales.

1	*(16-ounce) jar pineapple preserves or jam*
1	*teaspoon fresh orange zest*
3	*tablespoons whole-berry cranberry sauce (optional)*
1	*cup shredded coconut*

Place the pineapple preserves, fresh orange zest, and cranberry sauce, if using, in a microwave dish, and heat. Stir to blend. Add the coconut. Use immediately or keep in the refrigerator for up to one week. Reheat before using.

MAKES ENOUGH CHUTNEY TO GARNISH 24 PUMPKIN TAMALES

Buñuelo
New Year Pastry

*B*uñuelos cannot be made in advance. They must be eaten almost immediately after frying, when they virtually melt in your mouth in a tide of sheer luxury. Carlotta says that honey may be substituted for syrup, and also that it is possible to make the dough a few hours ahead.

2	*cups flour*
½	*teaspoon baking powder*
½	*teaspoon salt*
2	*eggs, beaten*
¼	*cup butter, softened*
¾	*cup milk, or water*
2	*cups oil, for frying*

SYRUP:

2	*cones piloncillo, crushed (or 4 cups dark brown sugar)*
1	*stick cinnamon*
2	*cups water*

GARNISH:

2	*cups heavy cream, whipped (sweetened, if desired)*
½	*cup chopped walnuts*

Sift together the flour, baking powder, and salt. Add the beaten eggs, butter, milk, and as much of the flour mixture as will be absorbed. Knead the dough. Divide it into 24 balls the size of limes. Press and roll the dough with a rolling pin to 4 or 5 inches in diameter. Heat the oil on high heat and fry each *buñuelo* on both sides until a delicate brown. Drain on paper towels.

To make the syrup, crumble the *piloncillo*, combine with the cinnamon and water, and boil until thickened. Pour over the hot *buñuelos*. Garnish with whipped cream and nuts, and serve immediately.

MAKES 24 BUÑUELOS

Bizcochuelos
Anise Cookies

Generally considered one of the essential Christmas cookies, anise-flavored *Bizcochuelos* are good to eat any time of the year. Carlotta points out that the dough can be made up to three days before you actually bake the cookies.

½	cup butter
½	sugar
1	egg
1	tablespoon brandy
½	teaspoon ground anise
1½	cups cake flour
1	teaspoon baking powder
¼	teaspoon salt
¼	cup light brown sugar
½	teaspoon ground cinnamon

Preheat the oven to 350°F (175°C). Cream together the butter and sugar. Add the egg and continue beating until fluffy. Add the anise and brandy. Combine the cake flour, baking powder, and salt. Gradually add the dry ingredients to the creamed mixture, mixing until well blended. Turn out the dough onto waxed paper, and knead lightly. Form the dough into a ball. Refrigerate the dough, wrapped in plastic, for at least 1 hour. Roll out the dough to ¼-inch thick. With a wreath-shaped cookie cutter or doughnut cutter, cut as many cookies as possible and place on an ungreased cookie sheet. Reroll the remaining dough and repeat the cutting process. Sprinkle the cookies with a mixture of the brown sugar and cinnamon. Bake for about 12 minutes, or until cookies are firm and starting to brown. Remove the cookies to a wire rack and cool before storing.

MAKES ABOUT 12 COOKIES

Cocadas
Macaroons

A light dessert suitable to have with coffee after a filling meal. Carlotta recalls that Monica served the children macaroons with hot chocolate.

3	*cups blanched almonds, coarsely chopped*
¾	*cups sugar*
10	*egg whites*

Preheat the oven to 350°F (175°C). Grind the almonds and sugar together. Gradually add the egg whites to make a soft dough. Drop by teaspoonfuls on a cookie sheet lined with waxed paper or parchment. Bake 8 to 10 minutes, or until set and showing tips of light brown.

MAKES 12 COOKIES

Empanadas de Manzana
Apple Turnovers

Empananadas dulces (sweet turnovers) are a specialty of nearly every good Mexican bakery. They a fine snack or dessert for a sit-down meal, but their self-contained nature makes them ideal take-along sweets for lunch boxes or picnics. Fillings can range from canned pumpkin pie mix to fruit preserves or apple sauce. This apple filling can be cooked for a long time until it is almost saucy, or more briefly, so the apples stay chunky (they will soften more while the empanadas bake).

	Empanada Pastry (page 144)
3	tart apples, peeled, cored, and chopped
½	cup sugar plus extra for sprinkling
	Scant ⅛ teaspoon salt
	Juice of 1 lemon
½	teaspoon cinnamon
¼	teaspoon ground cloves
1	egg (optional)
2	tablespoons water (optional)

Prepare Empanada Pastry. Preheat the oven to 400°F (200°C). Combine the apples, the ½ cup sugar, salt, lemon juice, cinnamon, and cloves in a saucepan. Cook over medium heat, stirring occasionally, until the apples are barely tender. Cut rounds of pastry about 4 inches in diameter. Place 1 or 2 tablespoons of the apple filling on the top half of the circle. Fold the bottom half up and over the filling, and press together the upper edges of the half-circle with the tines of a fork to seal. Prepare the egg wash, if desired, by beating together the egg and water.

Brush the empanadas with the egg wash, if desired, and sprinkle with the extra sugar. Place the filled empanadas on an ungreased baking sheet, and bake for 15 to 20 minutes, or until the pastry is nicely browned. Remove to a wire rack to cool, or serve warm.

MAKES 8 SERVINGS

Galletas
Mexican Wedding Cookies

Carlotta calls this "a timeless recipe for cookies so delicate they seem to pop and disappear in the mouth." It is customary to make enough so that guests at a wedding can take some home as a kind of edible thank-you gift for coming to the fiesta.

1	cup soft margarine, or butter
½	cup plus ¾ cup powdered sugar
1	teaspoon vanilla extract
2	cups all-purpose flour
¼	teaspoon salt
1	cup finely chopped, or coarsely ground, almonds

Preheat the oven to 325°F (165°C). In a large bowl beat together the margarine or butter, ½ cup of the powdered sugar, and vanilla until light and fluffy. Combine the flour, salt, and chopped almonds. Gradually, but quickly, add the flour mixture to the creamed mixture and mix on low speed just until partially blended. Turn the dough onto a board and knead by hand with a light touch until well blended. The less handling the better. Form into 1-inch balls. Place the balls on an ungreased cookie sheet and bake for 15 to 20 minutes until set, but not brown. Cool slightly, and then roll each ball in remaining ¾ cup powdered sugar. Cool completely and roll cookies a second time in the powdered sugar. Store in airtight containers, or freeze.

[Notita: The dough can be rolled to a ¼-inch thickness, and cut into small crescents, circles, or other shapes.]

[Chocolate variation: To make a chocolate version of Mexican Wedding Cookies, add an extra tablespoon of butter or margarine along with unsweetened cocoa. Combine the same amount of cocoa as powdered sugar (1¼ cups each, divided) in the batter as well as to the coating in which the baked cookies are rolled.]

MAKES 24 COOKIES

Galletitas de Almendra
Almond Cookies

This is an old, old recipe I found in my grandmother's hand-written recipe book," Carlotta reveals, remembering that they were among her favorite things to eat when she was a child.

1¾	cups all-purpose flour
¼	teaspoon salt
1	cup softened butter or margarine
1	plus 1 cup powdered sugar
1	teaspoon almond extract
¾	cup ground almonds
1	cup uncooked oats

Preheat the oven to 325°F (165°C). Combine the flour and salt. In a large bowl beat the butter or margarine with 1 cup powdered sugar until light and fluffy. Beat in the almond extract. Gradually stir in the flour and salt mixture, mixing well. Then stir in the ground almonds and oatmeal just until incorporated. Shape the dough into crescents using walnut-size balls of dough. Bake for 10 to 15 minutes on ungreased cookie sheets. Remove to a wire rack and cool. Roll the cookies in the additional cup of powdered sugar. Store tightly covered, or freeze.

MAKES ABOUT 36 COOKIES

Los Besos del Angel
Meringues

I believe meringues and macaroons are in Tucson's repertoire because of the many Jewish settlers of French and German cultural ancestry who have enriched the city for more than 100 years," Carlotta says. She adds that Tucson is one of the best places in the world to make meringues because of its nearly year-around humidity level of 10 to 12 percent. "Anyone who has ever struggled with flopped egg whites will love to make them in Tucscon."

6	*egg whites at room temperature*
½	*teaspoon cream of tartar*
1	*teaspoon almond extract*
1½	*cups sugar*

Preheat the oven to 225°F (110°C). Line a baking sheet with brown paper or parchment that has been buttered and floured. Beat the egg whites and cream of tartar until soft peaks form. Add the almond extract. Stir in the sugar gradually. Place the meringue mixture in a pastry bag and pipe rounds onto the prepared baking sheet. Quickly place in the oven for about 45 minutes, or until the meringues are dry. Cool completely, and store in an air-tight container for up to a week.

MAKES 6 MERINGUES

Drinks

(Bebidas)

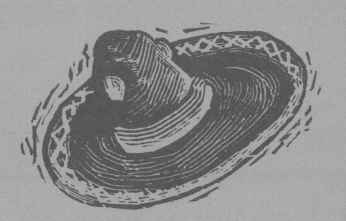

Travel around southern Arizona, especially in the summer months, and you come to realize the importance of *refrescos* (cool drinks) to help offset the desert heat. The variety of refreshing libations on local menus is truly wondrous, from the omnipresent rice milk known as *horchata* to unusual lemonades and flower-flavored pick-me-ups. Even brand-name soft drink connoisseurs have staked out Tucson as a place where it is possible to get bottled-in-Mexico Coca-Cola, which they consider infinitely superior to the US-bottled variety.

Chocolate Caliente
Beaten Hot Chocolate

This is one of the richest hot chocolates you will ever savor. Carlotta regretfully reminds us that the traditional recipe, which calls for separated raw eggs, is an at-your-own-risk proposition because of the possibility of salmonella. It is possible to use a pasteurized egg substitute in place of the yolks and simply forgo the lovely froth contributed by the fluffed raw egg whites.

---

4   tablespoons cocoa (or 4 squares Ibarra Mexican chocolate)

3   cups whole milk (or 12 ounces evaporated milk and 12 ounces water)

1   cup sugar
      Pinch of salt

3   eggs, separated

1   teaspoon vanilla extract
      Ground cinnamon, optional

Dissolve the cocoa in a small amount of water (or melt the chocolate squares over hot water). Place in a saucepan and stir in the milk (or evaporated milk and water), sugar, and salt. Cook over medium heat until the mixture comes to the boil. Beat the egg yolks until thick and lemon-colored. Beat the whites until stiff and fold them into the yolks. Add the vanilla. Add the egg mixture to the chocolate mixture. Whip with a molinillo (the traditional whisk made of decoratively carved wood) or a wire whisk and serve with a sprinkle of ground cinnamon.

MAKES 3 TO 6 SERVINGS

Horchata (Agua de Arroz)
Rice-Water Cooler

An indescribably refreshing beverage sold in restaurants and at fruit-juice stands all over Tucson, *Horchata* is believed to have magical powers to soothe everyone from colicky babies to cranky adults. As a special touch, offer a cinnamon stick in each glass to stir the *Horchata*.

1½	*plus 2 quarts water*
4	*cups rice*
	Cinnamon sticks (enough for each person)
1	*quart nonfat milk*
2	*cups sugar*
	Ground cinnamon or nutmeg (optional)

Soak the rice in the 1½ quarts water for 4 hours. Drain. A batch at a time, purée the rice in a blender with some of the milk. The rice will not be completely puréed, so strain the mixture well, discarding the hard bits of rice, and reserving the milky extract. Next, dissolve the sugar in the additional 2 quarts water. Combine with the rice and milk mixture. Refrigerate before serving. Serve over ice, and top with ground cinnamon or nutmeg, if desired.

MAKES 12 SERVINGS

Horchata de Coco
Coconut Drink

Carlotta did not want her children drinking sugary soft drinks; so she served them *Horchata de Coco* instead. She advises that the amount of sugar can be adjusted to taste.

1	*large coconut*
2	*quarts scalding water*
2	*cups sugar*
	Chopped ice

Grind and sift the coconut meat. Place in a heatproof container with the scalding water. When cold, strain. Add the sugar and chopped ice.

[Variation: Substitute 3 cups of watermelon pulp for the coconut to make a watermelon drink.]

MAKES ABOUT 3 QUARTS

Jamaica
Hibiscus Drink

Served hot or cold, Jamaica is made from the petals of the hibiscus plant, which give it a beautiful pink hue.

½	pound Jamaica petals (found in produce department)
1	plus 5 quarts water
2	cups sugar
	Ice
	Orange slices

Wash the Jamaica petals. Boil the 1 quart of water and add the Jamaica petals. Set aside for 2 hours. Strain; add the sugar and the remaining 5 quarts water. Serve with ice and orange slices.

MAKES ABOUT 6 QUARTS

Tamarindo
Tamarind Drink

A strange, fetching, refreshing drink that can be offered to guests as an after-dinner surprise. We have found it to be an ideal punctuation mark in the middle of a long, hot afternoon.

½   *pound tamarinds, peeled and cut in half*

2   *cups plus 5½ quarts water*

2   *cups sugar*

       Ice

       Mint sprigs, slices of lemon or orange

In a saucepan place the tamarinds with the 2 cups cold water. Bring to the boil. Reduce the heat and simmer gently for 15 minutes. When cool, remove the tamarinds. Strain the liquid into a large pitcher. Stir in the sugar. Add the remaining 5½ quarts water. Serve with ice and a sprig of mint or slices of lemon or orange.

MAKES ABOUT 6 QUARTS

Café de Olla
Mexican Coffee

This cinnamon-steeped beverage can be prepared in a drip-style coffee maker. To turn this into an after-dinner drink, add a splash of liqueur and whipped cream.

½	cup ground coffee
1	cinnamon stick (about 3 inches long) broken in half
1	small (3-ounce) cone piloncillo, chopped or 4 tablespoons firmly packed brown sugur
4	cups water

Place coffee in filter container of drip style pot. Scatter cinnamon and brown sugar or *piloncillo* over coffee. Brew with water.

MAKES 4 TO 6 SERVINGS

Alcoholic Beverages

(Bebidas Alcohólicas)

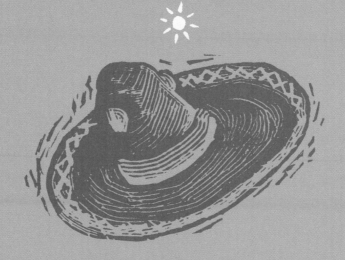

"¡Pa arriba, pa abajo, para centro, para dentro!"
(Up, down, center, and down the hatch!")

Sangría de Flores
Flores Family Wine Punch

It is Carlotta's contention that nothing adorns a glass of sangria quite as well as a few rose petals floating atop the wine.

1	bottle red burgundy wine
½	bottle of Presidente brandy
¾	cup orange juice
¾	cup grapefruit juice
¾	cup cranberry juice
	Juice of 4 limes

GARNISH:

1	cup chopped apple
1	cup chopped orange segments
1	cup chopped cantaloupe
1	cup rose petals (optional)

In a punch bowl, combine the wine, brandy, and orange, grapefruit, cranberry, and lime juices. Add the apple, orange, and cantaloupe, and the rose petals, if using, just before serving.

[Notita: To keep the punch cool without diluting it, freeze an extra quart of one of the juices in a ring mold. Add the frozen juice to the punch, and it will float prettily.]

MAKES 8 TO 10 CUPS

Rompope
Eggnog

The Flores family fondly remembers Christmas parties Monica threw for employees in the 1940s and 1950s. The libation of choice was egg nog—each serving accompanied by a cinnamon stick to stir it. Cookies were served on the side.

3	*cups of condensed milk*
3	*cups milk (2 percent or whole)*
6	*ounces of dark rum (optional)*
6	*egg yolks*
1	*pint heavy whipping cream*
8	*(6-inch long) fresh cinnamon sticks*
	Powdered nutmeg garnish

Place in a blender the milks, the egg yolks, and the rum if using and whip until the mixture is smooth and creamy. In a separate bowl whip the real heavy cream (if you want it to be sweeter add sugar to taste and fold into the cream as it is whipped). Serve this hot in mugs with a cinnamon stick, a dab of whipped cream, and some fresh powdered nutmeg.

(Notita: to avoid any possibility thereof, use pasteurized egg substitute in place of the eggs. The Rompope won't taste as good, but neither will you run the risk of falling ill.)

MAKES 9 CUPS

Margarita Mystique

Margarita Mystique

It was a thirst for power and wealth that brought the Spanish Conquistadors to Mexico in 1521. In the name of the crown, they conquered Mexico and instituted a tyrannical regime, one bent on bleeding the land of its wealth and natural resources. The Spanish inexorably changed the face of Mexico, influencing, among other things, its language, architecture, and social fabric.

The Spanish also brought with them the art and science of distillation, having themselves been introduced to distilling spirits in the eighth century. Arriving in Mexico, the Conquistadors found numerous Indian civilizations that made a fermented drink now known as *pulque* (pronounced pool-kay). Made since shortly after the time of Christ, this viscous, milky drink is thought to be the oldest alcoholic beverage in North America.

Pulque is made from the fermented sap of the agave, a succulent related to the lily or aloe of which there are an estimated 500 varieties indigenous to the Mexico and Sonoran desert. The syrupy sap, known as *aguamiel*, ferments naturally and is low in alcohol. The Spanish, long used to the pleasures of wine and brandy, found *pulque* wanting, and took to distilling the fermented juice of several species of agave. These rudimentary, herbaceous spirits were called agave or mescal wine.

In 1795 King Charles III of Spain granted the first license to the distillery owned by Jose Cuervo. Numerous other distilleries began operation in the early 1800s. Distillers began cultivating agaves in large numbers. As Mexico set out the long road to independence, in 1812 María Magdelena Ignacia, daughter of Josée María Guadalupe Cuervo, inherited the Cuervo family distillery. She married Vicente Albino Rojas, who promoted the family spirit to other Mexican states. Nearly twenty years later, General Santa Anna assumed control of the newly independent country, beginning a fifty-five-year period of civil upheaval and military conflict. It was a dangerous time for the people of Mexico, including the numerous distillers of mezcal wine.

During a relatively brief period of governmental and economic stability, Cuervo celebrated its first export to the United States along with recognition at the Chicago World's Fair in 1893. Shortly after that Mexico was again thrown into turmoil with the beginning of the revolution in 1910. The following decade was marred by violence and hardship. A democratic government was finally instituted in May 1920.

With the advent of the twentieth century, tequila as a category had emerged as a commodity on the world market. Mechanization greatly increased production, and bottling tequila widely broadened its sphere of influence. During the decade ending in 1910, the number of distilleries producing tequila grew from sixty-eight to eighty-seven. By 1931 worldwide demand for tequila was exceeding the industry's capability to produce it. In response the distillers decided amongst themselves to permit the addition of non-agave sugars to supplement the aguamiel. Reducing the percentage of agave in tequila significantly expanded production. And mixto tequila was born.

Tequila was one of the few spirits whose supply was not disrupted by World War II. In 1945 a record one million gallons of tequila were exported to the United States. With the return to normalcy after the war, however, other major spirits were once again readily available. Spirits such as gin, rum, Scotch, and brandy quickly returned to the popular forefront. The late forties also saw the emergence of vodka as a mainstream liquor in the U.S. With interest dwindling tequila nearly fell out of the market.

By 1948 worldwide consumption of tequila had dropped off dramatically. When exports to the United States and Europe all but stopped, it precipitated a wide spread financial crisis referred to as the Tequila Crash. The majority of distillers slashed production; the others ceased operations altogether. Although the tequila industry was experiencing a decline, the neighbors to the north were experiencing prosperity. It was during this time that some say the margarita was born and the tequila industry was saved.

Margarita Sames

San Antonio native Margarita Sames was a self-described socialite who, along with her husband Bill, owned a villa near the Flamingo Hotel in Acapulco, Mexico. The year was 1948 and times were good. The war had ended three years before and the country was experiencing a prolonged period of prosperity. For the rich and famous, Acapulco was an irresistible playground.

The Sames lived in Acapulco for part of the year. There they developed a close circle of friends, affectionately dubbed the "team." The cadre consisted of Fred MacMurray, Lana Turner, Nick Hilton, next door neighbor John Wayne, Joseph Drown, owner of the Hotel Bel-Air, and restauranteur Shelton McHenrie, owner of the Tail o' the Cock restaurant in Los Angeles.

This group of influential, high-profile friends was practically inseparable. They reveled in the festive, laid back attitude of Acapulco, spending their nights playing by the pool and downing a considerable number of cocktails. Lunch time was typically served somewhere around sunset. Margarita Sames had an effervescent personality and disarming smile. She was a social magnet and the unofficial leader of the group. The Sames house was the setting for many wild parties, raucous affairs that sometimes lasted days on end.

Shortly before Christmas 1948 Margarita Sames was challenged by several ranking members of the team to devise a new and exciting cocktail, something to break up their regimen of beer and Bloody Marys. Her initial attempts were loudly and unanimously rejected. After each round of successively worse drinks, her friends, this band of movie stars and distinguished businessmen, expressed their displeasure by tossing her in the pool.

Undaunted, a soaking wet Margarita Sames went back to work. She mixed together tequila and Cointreau with fresh lime juice. Having grown up in France, Sames was well-familiar with Cointreau, and after spending years vacationing in Mexico, she had developed an appreciation for Mexico's native spirit, tequila.

She tried several different formulations, however, some came out too sweet, some not sweet enough. Then she hit on what she thought was the perfect blend—one part Cointreau, three parts tequila, and one part lime juice. Knowing that most people drank tequila preceded by a lick of salt, she chose to garnish her cocktail with a rim of course salt.

She brought out a tray of champagne glasses brimming with her new creation. Her friends sipped heartily and the approval was overwhelming. They proclaimed it a triumph. It quickly became the group's signature cocktail, the main course and featured attraction during Christmas and New Year's Eve.

Sames credits the proliferation of the drink to her friend, John Wayne, Fred MacMurray, and Lana Turner. Her emissaries would go to restaurants and bars, tell the bartenders about the Margarita and order a few rounds. Soon it was a specialty at the Acapulco Airport. Nicky Hilton began promoting the cocktail at the bars in the popular Acapulco Hilton, as did Joe Drown at the Hotel Bel-Aire.

In the years following Margarita Sames remained a socialite in the international set. She continued serving her cocktail to her growing host of friends. She spent many afternoons sipping margaritas with Eleanor Roosevelt, and the legendary baseball manager John McGraw was a lifelong friend of the Sames and the Margarita.

In 1993 her friends threw Margarita Sames an eighty-second birthday party that lasted five days. The drink of choice . . . well, you can just imagine.

Black Forest Margarita
a.k.a. Black Cherry Margarita

	Cocktail or house specialty glass (salted rim and ice, optional)
1¼	*ounces Cuervo Gold tequila*
¾	*ounce cherry schnapps*
½	*ounce Rose's lime juice*
2	*ounces sweet-n-sour mix*
2	*ounces orange juice*
	Fresh lime wedge, for garnish

In a cocktail glass put the tequila, schnapps, lime juice, sweet-n-sour mix, and orange juice. Shake and strain. Garnish with the fresh lime wedge.

MAKES 1 PINT-GLASS SERVING

Sonoran Margarita

	Cocktail or specialty glass, chilled (salted rim and ice optional)
1¼	*ounces Cuervo Anejo tequila*
¾	*ounce Grand Marnier*
½	*ounce Rose's lime juice*
1½	*ounces sweet-n-sour mix*
	Fresh lime wedge, for garnish.

In a cocktail glass put the tequila, Grand Marnier, lime juice, and sweet-n-sour mix. Shake and strain. Garnish with lime wedge.

El Charro Margarita de Casa

The traditional El Charro method of serving a Margarita is over ice in a salt-rimmed glass (preferably a hand-blown, blue-rimmed glass). Many people like it frozen, i.e. combined with crushed ice rather than ice cubes; but this method of serving demands you drink it very fast, lest the ice melt quickly and water down the tequila.

Pieces of fresh peach or mango, or whole strawberries or raspberries may be offered in lieu of the more traditional wedge of lime.

½   part Cuervo Gold

½   part Cuervo Silver

2   parts Cuervo Margarita Mix

      Splash of Triple Sec

      Squeeze of lime juice

      Splash of orange juice

      Lime wedge, optional

Combine the Cuervo Gold, Cuervo Silver, Cuervo Margarita Mix, Triple Sec, and lime and orange juices, and serve over ice cubes in a salt-rimmed Margarita glass. Add the lime wedge, if using.

Margarita Splash

House specialty glass (salted rim, optional)
Ice
1¼   *ounces Cuervo Gold tequila*
½   *ounce Rose's triple sec*
1½   *ounces fresh lime juice*
1½   *ounces sweet-n-sour mix*
Club soda
Fresh lime wedge, for garnish

In a glass put the ice, tequila, triple sec, lime juice, and sweet-n-sour mix. Shake and strain. Fill the glass with the club soda. Garnish with the fresh lime wedge.

Raspberry Margarita

1½   *ounces Cuervo Gold tequila*
½   *ounce Rose's triple sec*
2   *ounces sweet-n-sour mix*

Mix together the tequila, triple sec, and sweet-and-sour mix. Blend with ice.

Charro ¡Mas-Tini!

¼   ounce José Cuervo La Familia

¼   ounce Cuervo 1800 Anejo Millennium Edition

¼   ounce José Cuervo Anejo

   Squeeze of lime

Serve chilled, up, in a Martini glass on a cocktail napkin with a lime garnish . . . or with an olive.

Charro Negro

10   to 12 ounces Coca-Cola or Pepsi-Cola

1¼   ounce Cuervo Tradicional tequila

   Squeeze of lime and garnish of lime wedge

Mix cola, tequila, and squeeze of lime in a tall glass (salted rim is optional). Garnish with lime wedge.

El Charro's Margaritas of the Day

Raymon Flores & Dave Guerrero

While purists might insist on the classic Margarita de Casa (page 195), Ray Flores has developed a full repertoire of variations on the theme and offers one each day at the restaurant. Here are some of his favorites:

MONDAY: Mango Bango

1¼	ounces Cuervo Tradicional tequila
¾	ounce crème de banana liqueur
1½	ounces sweet-n-sour mix
	Island Oasis mango juice
	Fruit, for garnish
	Whipped cream, for garnish

In a shaker combine the tequila, crème de banana, and sweet-n-sour mix. Fill the shaker with the mango juice and garnish with the fruit and whipped cream.

TUESDAY: 'Da Ba Da Bing!

1¼	ounces Cuervo 1800 Reposado tequila
¾	ounce amaretto
½	ounce triple sec or Citronge
½	ounce orange juice
2	ounces sweet-n-sour mix
	Orange wedge, for garnish
	Cherry, for garnish

Mix together the tequila, amaretto, triple sec, orange juice, and sweet-n-sour mix. Serve on the rocks or frozen in a pint glass garnished with the orange wedge and cherry.

WEDNESDAY: Menage-A-Cuervo

½   ounce Cuervo 1800 Reposado tequila

½   ounce Tradicional tequila

½   ounce Cuervo Gold tequila

Lime juice (sweet-n-sour)

Splash of orange juice

Lime wedge

Mix together the tequilas, lime juice, and orange juice. Serve on the rocks or frozen in a pint glass with a lime wedge for garnish.

THURSDAY: Raspberry José

Purple Haze
This is a layered margarita.

12   ounces frozen margarita

¼   shot plus ¼ shot raspberry liqueur

Pour in a small amount of the frozen margarita into the bottom of a glass; then pour in ¼ shot glass of the raspberry liqueur. Next slowly pour in more frozen margarita and the remaining ¼ shot glass of the raspberry liqueur. Then pour in the rest of the frozen margarita, and top it off with a float of the raspberry liqueur.

FRIDAY: ¡Toma! Apple Rita

1¼   ounces Cuervo Tradicional tequila

1   ounce Apple Pucker

2   to 3 ounces sweet-n-sour mix

Sprite or 7-Up

Lime wedge, for garnish

Mix in a glass the tequila, Apple Pucker, and sweet-n-sour mix. Fill with the Sprite. Serve on the rocks, or frozen in a pint glass with a lime wedge for garnish.

SATURDAY: Prickly Pear Rita

1-¼	ounces of Cuervo Tradicional tequila
½	ounce Rose's triple sec
½	ounce Rose's lime juice
¼	ounce grenadine
¾	ounce prickly pear juice
1½	ounces sweet-n-sour mix
	Ice
	Lime wedge, for garnish

Mix in a glass the tequila, triple sec, lime juice, grenadine, prickly pear juice, and sweet-n-sour mix. Blend with the ice. Serve on the rocks, or frozen in a pint glass with a lime wedge for garnish.

SUNDAY: Charro Cool-Aid

1¼	ounces of Cuervo 1800 Reposado tequila
½	ounce melon liqueur
1½	ounces peach schnapps
	Cranberry juice
	Fruit, for garnish

Mix in a glass the tequila and melon liqueur evenly with the peach schnapps. Fill the rest of the glass with the cranberry juice. Serve on the rocks, or frozen in a pint glass with the fruit for garnish.

Glossary

*

Aceite: Cooking oil

Aceituna: Olive oil

Achiote: A red-orange mixture of spices, it gets its color from the annto nut and is blended with Seville oranges. This can be found in block form in the specialty areas of supermarket ethnic aisles. This delectable mixture adds wonderful flavor to chicken, fish, and especially pork.

Adobo: A mixture of spices that are usually dried, containing garlic, cinnamon, and regional chiles mixed with vinegar

Agua: Water

Aguacate: Avocado or alligator pear—dark, coarse skinned ones taste better

Ajo: Garlic

Albóndigas: Meatballs

Al horno: Oven-baked

Ancho: A poblano chile that has been dried and has turned a black-red color

Antojito: An hors d'oeuvre or small snack food

Arroz: Rice

Asar: To roast or broil

Azúcar: Sugar

Barbacoa: Barbecued meat

Borracho: Cooked with beer or wine (means "drunk")

Buñuelo: Puffy, sweet, deep-fried pastry

Burro: Large flour tortilla wrapped around a filling

Calabaza: Squash, pumpkin

Caldo: Soup, broth

Caliente: Hot to the touch

Camarón: Shrimp

Camote: Sweet potato

Canela: Cinnamon

Capirotada: Spicy bread pudding served during Lent (means "a little bit of everything")

Carne: Meet, specifically beef

Carne seca: Dried beef jerky, shredded and spiced

Cazuela: A stew pot (at El Charro a hearty bowl of "dry" beef soup)

Cebolla: Onion

Cerveza: Beer

Ceviche: Salad made of fish "cooked" in lime juice

Chalupa: Corn masa tart, fried, then topped with meat, fish, beans, or vegetables (means "canoe")

Chilaquiles: Corn tortilla pieces covered with enchilada sauce and cheese and baked in a casserole

Chile: The Spanish spelling for pepper (The Spanish interepreted the sound "chil" used by the Aztecs for hot peppers. Other writers choose *chili*, insisting *chile* is the name of a country.)

Chimichanga: Deep-fried burro (means "thingamajig")

Chorizo: Pork or beef sausage

Chuleta: Chop or cutlet

Cilantro: Coriander or Chinese parsley

Coco: Coconut

Comal: Heavy, round griddle for baking tortillas

Con: With or as

Ejote: String bean

Elote: Corn (sometimes *helote*)

Empanada: Pastry turnover

Enchilada: A corn tortilla dipped in red chile sauce and filled with just about anything and topped with more sauce

Enrollado: Rolled

Escabeche: Pickle

Fideos: Vermicelli (thin pasta)

Flan: Baked custard with caramel coating

Flauta: Corn tortilla tightly rolled around a filling then deep fried (means "flute")

Frijoles: Beans, usually pinto beans

Gallina: Hen

Garbanzo: Chick pea

Gazpacho: Cold, spicy tomato soup

Granada: Pomegranate

Guacamole: Mashed avocado salad or dip

Guajolote: Turkey (in Mexico)

Harina: Wheat flour

Hoja: Corn husk, used to wrap tamales (sometimes *oja*)

Hongo: Mushroom

Huevo: Egg (also *blanquillo*)

Jamón: Ham

Jícama: A crisp, white, edible root

Kahlúa: Coffee-flavored liqueur made in Mexico

Lechuga: Lettuce

Lima: Lime

Limón: Lemon

Maíze: Corn

Mano: A piece of volcanic rock used to grind food (also means "hard" or "hand")

Manteca: Lard

Mantequilla: Butter

Mariscos: Shellfish

Masa: Dough

Menudo: Tripe soup

Metate: Slab of volcanic rock on three legs used for grinding corn

Miel: Honey

Molcajete: Volcanic rock shaped like a bowl used to grind food

Molé: a mixture of seeds, nuts, spices, and herbs. No flour is used to thicken a true molé.

Molinillo: Hot chocolate beater, usually made of beautifully carved wood

Naranja: Orange

Nixtamal: Hominy, raw corn grains soaked in lime and ground to make a dough for tortillas, tamales, and chalupas

Nopales: Prickly-pear cactus pads cooked and used in fresh salads or cooked as a vegetable

O: Or

Olla: Clay pot, in which beans are simmered

Pan: Bread

Pastel: Pie

Pechuga de pollo: Breast of chicken

Pepino: Cucumber

Picadillo: Meat hash (literally means "cut up")

Picante: Hot to the taste buds

Pico de gallo: Rooster's beak — It refers playfully to the hot-and-spicy mixture we sprinkle over fresh fruit (page 000). In some areas, including Tucson, pico de gallo refers to a tomato-and-chile salsa.

Piloncillo: Brown sugar formed into a cone for commercial sale

Pimiento: Red pepper

Piñones: Pine nuts (also *pignoles*)

Pipián: a sauce that is made of basic red or green chili sauce.

Poblano: A variety of green chile

Pollo: Chicken

Postre: Dessert

Quelites: Spinach (sometimes any green-leaf vegetable)

Quesadilla: Grilled-cheese sandwich made with a tortilla

Queso: Cheese

Rábano: Radish

Rajas: Thin strips, as in thin strips of chile

Recado: a mixture of dried spices usually softened with vinegar.

Relleno: Stuffed

Repollo: Cabbage

Ristra: String of dried red chiles (also *sarta*)

Sal: Salt (*sin sal* means without salt)

Salsa: Sauce

Sangría: A drink made of red wine, brandy, sugar, oranges, lemons, and apples

Seco: Dry

Sofrito: Spanish seasoning mix — cilantro, parsley, garlic, onion, and bell peppers, chopped and packed in jars — that will last about 3 weeks.

Sopa: Soup

Sopa seca: Literally, a "dry soup," indicating a dish made with rice or a pasta that absorbs most of the liquid

Taco: A *U*-shaped corn tortilla with filling

Tamal (pl. tamales): A corn husk filled with masa, meat, or beans

Tatemar: To roast, peel, and seed green chiles

Tejolote: Pestle

Tequila: Distilled liquor made from agave (century plant)

Topopo: A salad shaped like a volcano or pyramid

Torta: Pie or pastry; omelet

Tortilla: A thin, flat bread made from either wheat flour (harina) or corn masa (nixtamal)

Tostada: Toasted; specifically, toasted tortillas

Totopos: Corn tortillas cut into triangles and fried in lard; also known as *tortilla chips*

Totopitos: Our name for the same totopos, but cut into sticks and fried for garnish on soups and salads

Dry Rubs: A natural with foods that have a high moisture content such as beef and pork steaks and roasts. Rubs are like herb bouquet garni bundles. Make a few of your favorites, and keep them by your stove. The one ingredient that goes in all rubs is salt. I prefer to use Kosher salt, and the rest is up to your personal taste.

One of my all time favorite rubs:

1 cup Kosher salt
½ cup garlic powder
2 tablespoons cracked black pepper
2 tablespoons paprika
2 tablespoons Mexican oregano

Infused: An overused word, but, nonetheless, it says it all. Instead of infusing butter or margarine with dill, garlic, or parsley, try adding it to your favorite salsa. Mix the salsa with your favorite spread, store and use it on your favorite bread, or when you pan fry, grill, or baste.

You will be happy that you have taken the extra steps to create rubs, recados, marinades, and herb bundle bouquets, because they all make cooking more foods easier and extremely delicious.

Index

Boldface indicates feature story

A
Achiote paste, 149
Agave nectar, 164
Albóndigas (Meatball Soup), 39
Almendrado, 156–57
Anaheim chiles, 13, 14, 15, 16, 28, 44, 45, 50, 60, 62, 69, 70, 71, 79-80, 81, 83, 89, 101, 119, 120, 138, 140, 143
Ancho chiles, 82
Anise, 165, 169
Apples, 115, 145, 171, 185
Apricot, dried, 127
Apricot preserves, 127
Arroz con Fruta (Rice with Fruit), 57
Arroz con Leche (Rice Pudding), 159
Arroz con Plátanos (White Rice with Bananas), 56
Arroz Estilo El Charro (El Charro Rice with Tomato), 55
Artichokes, 128
Avocado, 13, 15, 47, 101, 103, 109, 114, 125
Azúcar Dulce (Sugar Candy), 163

B
Bananas, 56, 61, 155
Barbacoa (Barbecued Beef), 138
Basic Vinaigrette, 106, 108, 109, 115
Beans:
  Canned:
    Pinto, 34, 35, 45, 66, 67, 69

  Refried, 15, 34, 35, 109
Beef:
  Brisket:
    Red Chile Tamales, 26–27,
  Ground:
    Albóndigas, 39
    Beef Tacos, 136
    Beef Turnovers, 144
    Chorizo, 148
    Hash, 145
  Roast:
    Barbecued Beef, 138
    Green Chile and Beef Stew, 140
    Machaca, 143
    Red Chile and Beef Stew, 141
  Shredded:
    Grilled Meat Tortilla, 35
    Quesadilla, 14
  Steak:
    Grilled Skirt Steak, 139
Bell peppers, red and/or green, 15, 35, 47, 50, 52, 74, 115, 120, 121, 132
Berenjena y Cilantro Crema (Eggplant with Cilantro Cream), 58
Bizcochuelos (Anise Cookies), 169
Black Forest Margarita (a.k.a. Black Cherry Margarita), 194
Bouquet Garni, **91–92**
Broth (*see soup stock*)
Buñuelo (New Year Pastry), 168
Burros, 34, 35
Burros (aka Burritos), **33**

C
Cabbage, 23, 102, 135, 136
Cactus, 107
Café de Olla (Mexican Coffee), 182
Cajeta de Piña (Pineapple Chutney), 167
Calabacitas con Queso (Squash with
   Cheese), 60
Calabaza Dulce (Sweet Banana Squash), 61
Caldo de Queso (Cheese and Potato Soup),
   44
Calendars, **64-65**
Cantaloupe, 185
Capirotada (Lenten Bread Pudding), 158
Carlotta's Calabaza (Pumpkin) Pan, 21
Carlotta's Ensalada de Espinaca (Spinach
   Salad), 114
Carmen Miranda's M. G. Special, 10
Carne Asada (Grilled Skirt Steak), 139
Carne Seca, **142**
Carne Verde (Green Chile & Beef Stew), 140
Carnitas de Puerco (Shredded Pork), 147
Carrots, 10, 43, 50, 78, 147
Cayenne pepper, 78, 131, 164
Celery, 43, 74, 101, 108, 128, 145
Ceviche (Seafood Salad), 101
Charro, 1-2,
Charro Mas-Tini, 197
Charro Negro, 197
Cheeses:
   Cheddar, 7, 8, 23, 34, 35, 119
   Cojita, 68, 103, 128
   Cottage, 28
   Feta, 16, 74
   Jack, 16, 109, 114, 125, 158
   Longhorn, 13, 15, 16, 17, 23, 28, 44, 52,
      60, 62 ,67, 125, 136
   Mexican, 16, 28, 44, 46, 62, 67, 69, 71,
      109, 114, 115, 119, 132, 135, 158
   Monterrey Jack, 47, 119
   Panela, 14, 46

Cherry Tom., Mint, and Cucumber Salsa, 77
Chicken:
   Chicken and Pasta, 132
   Chicken Pasta Salad with Tequila, 108
   Chicken Tacos, 135
   Chicken with Pumpkin Seeds and Red
      Chile Sauce, 134
   80th Anniversary Special Chicken, 128
   Grilled Chicken in Spirits, 130
   Grilled Meat Burrito, 35
   Lemon Chicken with Green Olives, 133
   New Year's Wish Chicken, 127
   Quesadilla, 14
   Rolled Enchiladas with Chicken, 125
   Speedy Chicken in Peanut Sauce, 126
   Tortilla Crusted Chicken, 131
   Volcano Salad Jalisco-style, 109
Chile Colorado/Chile con Carne (Red Chile
   and Beef Stew), 141
Chile Peppers, description of, 72–73:
Chile Primer, **72-73**
Chiles de arbol, 88
Chiles Rellenos (Stuffed Chiles), 62
Chiliquiles (Egg & Cheese Casserole), 8
Chimichanga, 36
Chipotle chiles, 16, 51, 78, 150
Chocolate Caliente (Hot Chocolate), 177
Chocolate, Mexican, 82, 177
Chorizo (Sausage), 148
Chuletas de Puerco con Olivas y Naranjas
   (Pork Chops with Olives and Oranges), 146
Cilantro and Green Cabbage Slaw, 102
Cinco de Mayo, **96-97**
Cocadas (Macaroons), 170
Cocoa, 162, 177
Coconut, 116, 155, 166, 167, 179
Corn:
   Baked Cod, Enchilada Style, 119
   Chicken Pasta Salad with Tequila, 108
   Chiliquiles, 8

Cornbread, 22
Corn Salad, 106
Green Corn Tamales, 28
Mashed Potato Soup, 51
Posole, 45
Squash and Pumpkin Soup, 42
Squash with Cheese, 60
Corn husks, 26–27
Corn Masa (Masa de elote):
  description of, 20
  Enchiladas Sonorenses, 23
  Red Chile Tamales, 26–27
Corn Tortilla:
  Beef Tacos, 136
  Chicken Tacos, 135
  Corn Chips and Strips, 113
  description of, 31
  Rolled Enchiladas with Chicken, 125
  Shrimp Tacos, 123
  Tortilla Soup, 47
  Volcano Salad Jalisco-style, 109
Corn Tortilla Chips:
  Cheese Fondue, 16
  Chiliquiles, 8
  Los Chacos, 15
  Mashed Potato Soup, 51
  Molé Poblano, 82
  Shrimp Salad with Tequila, 103
  Tomato Soup, 41
  Tortilla Crusted Chicken, 131
Costillas de Puerco en Salsa Chipotle (Pork
  Ribs in Pepper Sauce), 150
Costillas de Puerco Estilo Pibil-Sin Ojas (Ribs
  with Mango & Fresh Mint Salsa), 148
Cucumbers, 77, 102, 103
Cuervo, Jose, 189

D
Day of the Dead, **124**

E
Eggplant, 58
Eggs:
  Almond Meringue Pudding, 156
  Beaten Hot Chocolate, 177
  Caramel Custard, 160
  Chiliquiles, 8
  Eggnog, 186
  Good Morning Tucson Burrito, 7
  Macaroons, 170
  Meringues, 174
  Rice Pudding, 159
  Stuffed Chiles, 62
  Three Kings Bread, 165
  Tomato Soup, 41
  Yazmin's Choco Flan, 162
Ejotes con Chile Colorado (String Beans
  with Red Chile Sauce), 63
El Charro Frijoles Refritos, 67
El Charro Margarita de Casa, 195
El Charro Red Enchilada Sauce, 90
El Charro's Margaritas of the Day, 198–199
Empanadas de Carne (Beef Turnovers), 144
Empanadas de Manzana (Apple), 171
Enchiladas Sonorenses (Flat Corn Masa
  Patties with Red Chile Sauce), 23
Ensalada de Camaron con Tequila (Shrimp
  Salad with Tequila), 103
Ensalada de Elote (Corn Salad), 106
Ensalada de Noche Buena (Christmas Eve
  Salad), 115
Ensalada de Nopales (Pear Salad), 107
Ensalada de Pasta con Pollo y Salsa de Tequila
  (Chicken Pasta Salad with Tequila), 108
Escabeche (Vegetable Pickle), 78

F
Flan (Caramel Custard), 160
Jules Flin, 49, 161

Flin, Monica, ix, 4, 10, 46, 49, 64, 85, 96, 97, 112, 124, 137, 161, 186

Flores, Candace, xii,

Flores, Carlotta, xii, 14, 24, 26, 29, 38, 45, 54, 56, 65, 81, 96, 97, 100, 104, 111, 132, 136, 137, 149, 174, 177, 179,

Flores, Marques, xii

Flores, Ray Jr., xii, 4, 59, 198

Flores, Ray Sr., xii, 1, 30, 64, 67,

Flour Tortillas:
  Eggplant with Cilantro Cream, 58
  Good Morning Tucson Burritos, 7
  Grilled Meat Burrito, 35
  How to make, **29–32**
  Quesadilla, 14
  Tostada Grande, 17
  Vegetarian Burrito, 34

Frijoles de la Olla (Whole Beans), 66

G

Galletas (Mexican Wedding Cookies), 172

Galletitas de Almendra (Almond), 173

Good Morning Tucson Burrito, 7

Grapefruit juice, 185

Grapes, 114, 115, 127

Green beans, 63

Green Chile Preparation, **79-80**

Green chiles:
  Cherry Tomato, Mint, and Cucumber Salsa, 77
  Chicken Pasta Salad with Tequila, 108
  Chiliquiles, 8
  80th Anniversary Special Chicken, 128
  Infused Hot Pepper Vinegar, 94
  Shellfish Soup, 43
  Shrimp Doblado, 121
  Squash and Pumpkin Soup, 42
  Tortilla Soup, 47

Grilled Meat Burrito, 35

Guacamole (Avocado Dip), 13

H

Haunted Basement, the, **161**

Hongos (Mushrooms), 68

Horchata (Agua de Arroz) (Rice-Water Cooler), 178

Horchata de Coco (Coconut Drink), 179

Hot Pepper Oil, 94

I

Ice cream, 155

Infused Hot Pepper Vinegar, 94

J

Jalapeño peppers:
  Barbecued Beef, 138
  Cheese Fondue, 16
  Cornbread, 22
  Corn Salad, 106
  Los Chachos, 15
  Prickly Pear Salad, 107
  Quesadilla, 14
  Salmon with Cilantro Pesto Sauce, 122
  Savory Jalapeño Stuffing, 74
  Shrimp Salad with Tequila, 103
  Shrimp Tacos, 123
  Volcano Salad Jalisco-style, 109
  Jamaica (Hibiscus Drink), 180

Jicama, 78

L

Las Charras Enchiladas de Pollo (Rolled Enchiladas with Chicken), 125

Lent at El Charro, **111-112**

Los Besos del Angel (Meringues), 174

Los Chachos (Corn Tortilla Chips with Melted Cheese), 15

M

Machaca (Carne Seca Substitute), 143

Margarita Mystique, **187-193**

Mariachi Music, **85-87**
Mexican Independence Day, **59,** 112
Mushrooms:
   Chicken and Pasta, 132
   Grilled Meat Burrito, 35
   Mushrooms, 68
   Vegetarian Burrito, 34

N
Nachos, 30
Nectarines, 116
Nuts, 61, 159, 165

O
Oatmeal, 173
Oil, chile, 103, 108
Oil, olive, 122
Olives, green:
   Barbecued Beef, 138
   Chicken and Pasta, 132
   Enchiladas Sonorenses, 23
   Lemon Chicken with Green Olives, 133
   Los Chachos, 15
   Red Chile Tamales, 26–27
   Volcano Salad Jalisco-style, 109
Olives, stuffed:
   Chicken Pasta Salad with Tequila, 108
   Eggplant with Cilantro Cream, 58
   Pork Chops with Olives and Oranges, 146

P
Pasta:
   Chicken and Pasta, 132
   Chicken Pasta Salad with Tequila, 108
   Vermicelli (fideos) Soup, 52
Peanut butter, 126
Pechuga de Pollo em Pipián Rápido
   (Speedy Chicken in Peanut Sauce), 126
Pechugas con Chorizo del Aniversario
   (80th Anniversary Chicken), 128–129

Pescado en Estilo de Enchilada (Baked Cod,
   Enchilada Style), 119
Pescado Viscayena (Fish Fillets with
   Vegetables), 120
Picadillo (Hash), 145
Pico de Charro (Chunky Green Chile and
   Tomato Sauce), 83
Pico de Gallo, 98, 114, 116
Pimientos, 106
Pine nuts, 71, 122, 144
Plátanos de Hacienda (House Bananas), 155
Plato de Fruta (Fruit Platter), 116
Pollo Borracho (Chicken in Spirits), 130
Pollo en Pipián (Chicken with Pumpkin
   Seeds and Red Chile Sauce), 134
Pollo Limón y Olivas Verdes (Lemon
   Chicken with Green Olives), 133
Pollo Próspero Año (New Year's Wish
   Chicken), 127
Pollo y Fideo (Chicken and Pasta), 132
Pomegrante, 115
Pork:
   Chops, 146
   Ham, 7
   Ribs, 149, 150, 151
   Roast, 26-27, 45, 147
   Sausage, 128
Posole (Pork and Hominy Soup), 45
Potatoes:
   Cheese and Potato Soup, 44
   Enchiladas Sonorenses, 23
   Fish Fillets with Vegetables, 120
   Fried Potatoes and Chiles, 70
   Good Morning Tucson Burritos, 7
   Green Chile and Beef Stew, 140
   Hash, 145
   Mashed Potato Soup, 51
   Mixed-Pepper Bisque, 50
   Puerco Adobado (Pork Ribs with Red
      Chile), 151

Pulque, 189–90
Pumpkin:
  Pumpkin Bread, 21
  Squash and Pumpkin Soup, 42
  Sweet Pumpkin Tamales, 166
Pumpkin seeds, 134

Q
Quelites con Frijoles (Spinach with
  Beans), 69
Quesadilla (Mexican Grilled Cheese
  Sandwich), 14

R
Radishes:
  Beef Tacos, 136
  Chicken Tacos, 135
  Cilantro with Green Cabbage Slaw, 102
  Enchiladas Sonorenses, 23
Rajas con Crema y Piñones (Creamed
  Green Chiles with Pine Nuts), 71
Raspberry Margarita, 196
Red peppers:
  Chicken with Pumpkin Seeds and Red
    Chile Sauce, 134
  Chili Paste, 84
  El Charro Red Enchilada Sauce, 90
  El Charro Rice with Tomato, 55
  Grilled Skirt Steak, 139
  Hot Pepper Oil, 94
  Infused Hot Pepper Vinegar, 94
  Mexican Sausage, 148
  Posole, 45
  Red Chile Tamales, 26
  Ribs with Mango & Fresh Mint Salsa, 149
  Seasoning Mix, A, 98
  Shellfish Soup, 43
  Shrimp Salad with Tequila, 103
  Relleno de Jalapeño, 74
Rice:

Albóndigas, 39
El Charro Rice with Tomato, 55
Grilled Meat Burrito, 35
Rice Flavored with Fruit, 57
Rice Pudding, 159
Rice-Water Cooler, 178
Vegetarian Burrito, 34
White Rice with Bananas, 56
Rompope (Eggnog), 186
Rosca de Reyes (Three Kings Bread), 165

S
Salmón con Salsa de Cilantro Pesto (Salmon
  with Cilantro Pesto Sauce), 122
Salsa Adobo (Chile Paste), 84
Salsa de Mango (Mango Salsa), 81
Salsa para Tacos (Taco Sauce), 88
Salsa Verde Para Enchiladas (Green
  Enchilada Sauce), 89
Salsa, description of, 76
Sames, Margarita, 191-193
Sangría de Flores (Flores Family Wine
  Punch), 185
Sauces:
  Adobo, 84
  Green enchilada, 89
  Pico de Charro, 83
  Red enchilada, 90
  Spicy Tomato Sauce, 128–29
  Taco, 88
Seafood:
  Cod (or firm other white fish):
    Baked Cod, Enchilada Style, 119
  Fish Fillets with Vegetables, 120
  Salmon with Cilantro Pesto Sauce, 122
  Seafood Salad, 101
  Shellfish Soup, 43
  Shrimp:
    Shrimp Doblado, 121
    Shrimp Salad with Tequila, 103

Shrimp Taco, 123
Shrimp Doblado, 121
Sonoran Margarita, 194
Sopa de Camote y Calabasa (Sweet Potato and Pumpkin Soup), 42
Sopa de Campanas Mixtas (Mixed-Pepper Bisque), 50
Sopa de Marisco (Shellfish Soup), 43
Sopa de Purée de Papas (Mashed Potato Soup), 51
Sopa de Tomate (Tomato Soup), 41
Sopa de Tortilla (Tortilla Soup), 47
Sopa Seca de Fideo (Vermicelli Soup), 52
Soup Stock:
    Albóndigas, 39
    Cheese and Potato Soup, 44
    Chicken with Pumpkin Seeds and Red Chile Sauce, 134
    description of, 38
    El Charro Rice with Tomato, 55
    Garlic Soup, 46
    Green Enchilada Sauce, 89
    Mashed Potato Soup, 51
    Mixed-Pepper Bisque, 50
    Molé Poblano, 82
    Posole, 45
    Speedy Chicken in Peanut Sauce, 126
    Squash and Pumpkin Soup, 42
    Tomato Soup, 41
    Tortilla Soup, 47
    Vermicelli Soup, 52
Spiced Zucchini Muffins, 9
Spinach:
    Shrimp Salad with Tequila, 103
    Spinach and Beans, 69
    Spinach Salad, 114
    Vegetarian Burrito, 34
Spirits:
    Beer, 130
    Brandy, 46, 185

Liqueur, Kahlúa, 160
Rum, 155, 186
Sherry, 134
Red burgundy, 185
Tequila:
    Black Forest Margarita, 194
    'Da Ba Da Bing!, 198
    Charro Cool-Aid, 200
    Charro Mas-Tini!, 197
    Charro Negro, 197
    Chicken Pasta Salad with Tequila, 108
    El Charro Margarita de Casa, 195
    Mango Bango, 198
    Margarita Splash, 196
    Menage-A-Cuervo, 199
    Prickly Pear Rita, 200
    Raspberry José, 199
    Raspberry Margarita, 196
    Shrimp Salad with Tequila, 103
    Sonoran Margarita, 194
    Toma! Apple Rita, 199
Triple sec, 103
White wine, 46, 148
Squash:
    Chicken Pasta Salad with Tequila, 108
    Mixed-Pepper Bisque, 50
    Squash with Cheese, 60
Strawberry Vinegar, 95
Super Bowl Fundido con Sabores de Chiles (Cheese Fondue with Chiles), 16
Sugar, brown, 61, 158, 163, 165, 168, 182
Sugar, powdered, 165, 172, 173
Sweet potatoes, 42

T
Tacos de Camarón (Shrimp Tacos), 123
Tacos de Carne (Beef Tacos), 136
Tacos de Pollo (Chicken Tacos), 135
Tamales de Calabaza (Sweet Pumpkin Tamales), 166–67

Tamales de Chile Colorado (Red Chile Tamales), 26–27
Tamales de Elote (Green Corn Tamales), 28
Tamales:
  description: **24–25**
  Green Corn Tamales, 28
  Red Chile Tamales, 26–27
Tamarindo (Tamarind Drink), 181
Tequila-Based Dessert Syrup, 164
Thingamajig, the Great, **36**
Tomatoes, fresh:
  Barbecued Beef, 138
  Cheese and Tomato Soup, 44
  Cherry Tomato, Mint, and Cucumber Salsa, 77
  Chunky Green Chile & Tomato Sauce, 83
  Corn Salad, 106
  80th Anniversary Special Chicken, 128
  Green Chile and Beef Stew, 140
  Grilled Meat Burrito, 35
  Guacamole, 13
  Hash, 145
  Los Chachos, 15
  Machaca, 143
  Mango Salsa, 81
  Molé Poblano, 82
  Prickly Pear Salad, 107
  Shrimp Salad with Tequila, 103
  Shrimp Tacos, 123
  Squash with Cheese, 60
  Tortilla Soup, 47
  Vegetarian Burrito, 34
  Vermicelli Soup, 52
  Volcano Salad Jalisco-style, 109
  Whole Beans, 66
Tomatoes, canned:
  Chicken and Pasta, 132
  Shellfish Soup, 43
  Shrimp Doblado, 121
  Taco Sauce, 88

Tomato sauce/purée:
  Chicken and Pasta, 132
  El Charro Rice with Tomato, 55
  Taco Sauce, 88
  Tomato Soup, 41
  Vermicelli Soup, 52
Topopo a la Jalisciense (Volcano Salad Jalisco-style), 109
Tortillas:
  description of, **29-31**
  Tortilla Crusted Chicken, 131
  Tortillas de Harina (Flour Tortillas, 32
Tostada Grande de Tucson (Original Large Cheese Crisp), 17
Tostada grande, how to make, 12
Totopos y Totopitos (Corn Chips and Strips), 113
Tucson Timeline, **48-49**

V
Vegetarian Burrito, 34
Vinegar, 145, 151
Vinegar, balsamic, 114
Vinegar cider, 139
Vinegar, chile, 108
Vinegar, wine, 148
Vinegar, white, 94, 95, 101
Virgin of Guadalupe, the, 64, **104-105**

W
World War II Hamburgers, **137**

Y
Yazmin's Choco Flan, 162

Z
Zucchini:
  Spiced Zucchini Muffins, 9